Cooking Class

73 Fun Recipes Kids Will Love to Make (and Eat!)

Deanna F. Cook

Storey Publishing

The mission of Storey Publishing is to serve our customers by publishing practical information that encourages personal independence in harmony with the environment.

EDITED BY Lisa H. Hiley
ART DIRECTION AND BOOK DESIGN BY Jessica Armstrong
TEXT PRODUCTION BY Jennifer Jepson Smith

COVER PHOTOGRAPHY BY © Carl Tremblay, front (2nd f.b.r., b.c.l. & r., 2nd f.t.l., t.r., m.l., t.l.), back (author, b.l., b.r., t.l., t.m.r.); © John Polak, back (c.m.); © Julie Bidwell Photography, front (b.r., m.r., t.m.l), back (t.m.l., t.r.); © marcin jucha/Shutterstock.com, front (background); © swavo/Shutterstock.com, front (b.r.)
INTERIOR PHOTOGRAPHY BY © Julie Bidwell Photography, 4, 5, 10, 11 l., 12–21, 24–28, 29 l., 30–39, 46–49, 52–61, 66–72, 73 b., 76, 78–83, 86, 87 m.l. & b.l., 89–91, 94–95, 98–109, 111 b. (all), 112–115, 120–121, 122 (angel hair, farfalle, ziti), 123, 126–137, 140–143, 148–157, 162–163, 166–173; © Carl Tremblay, 6, 8, 22, 40–45, 50, 62–65, 73 t., 74–75, 77, 84–85, 87 all but m.l. & b.l., 88, 92–93, 96–97, 110, 111 t., 116–118, 124–125, 138–139, 144–147, 158–161, 164–165
ADDITIONAL PHOTOGRAPHY BY © John Polak, 176; Mars Vilaubi © Storey Publishing, 29 all but l., 122 (fettucine, letters, penne, rotini); © VeronikaSmirnaya/Shutterstock.com, 11 r.
FOOD STYLING BY Joy Howard
ILLUSTRATIONS BY © Emily Balsley

Text © 2015, 2024 by Deanna F. Cook

Storey books may be purchased in bulk for business, educational, or promotional use. Special editions or book excerpts can also be created to specification. For details, please contact your local bookseller or the Hachette Book Group Special Markets Department at special.markets@hbgusa.com.

Storey Publishing
210 MASS MoCA Way
North Adams, MA 01247
storey.com

Storey Publishing is an imprint of Workman Publishing, a division of Hachette Book Group, Inc., 1290 Avenue of the Americas, New York, NY 10104. The Storey Publishing name and logo are registered trademarks of Hachette Book Group, Inc.

Distributed in Europe by Hachette Livre, 58 rue Jean Bleuzen, 92 178 Vanves Cedex, France
Distributed in the United Kingdom by Hachette Book Group, UK, Carmelite House, 50 Victoria Embankment, London EC4Y 0DZ

ISBNs: 978-1-63586-779-4 (paper over board with 3 sticker sheets and 3 cardstock sheets); 978-1-63586-785-5 (fixed format EPUB); 978-1-63586-906-4 (fixed format PDF); 978-1-63586-907-1 (fixed format Kindle)

Printed in Dongguan, China by R. R. Donnelley on paper from responsible sources
10 9 8 7 6 5 4 3 2 1

APS

Library of Congress Cataloging-in-Publication Data on file

Dedicated to my girls,
ELLA & MAISIE

HELLO, COOKING FRIENDS!

I'm happy you picked up a copy of *Cooking Class* and that you're ready to start cooking! When I was your age, I loved looking at cookbooks and finding new recipes to try (with the last name of Cook, I grew up thinking, "I should cook!"). My daughters like to spend time in the kitchen with their friends, and they inspired me to collect the recipes in this cookbook. I hope you like the recipes as much as they do.

It was fun working with so many great kids to make all the food for the book. I want to thank them all for their time and for the yummy food they made. Thank you, Abby, Adia, Alex, Amelia, Arden, Aria, Ariana D., Arianna R.F., Asha, Audrey, August, Brady, Caleb, Chloe, Christian, Coco, Conor, Emilie, Ella, Ernnie, Finn, Grace, Inez, Iris, James, Jimmy, Jovan, Kelly, Lauren, Leila, Louisa, Maceo, Maddie, Maisie, Malia, Margaux, Mia, Nat, Phin, Pranav, Reyna, Rohin, Ruby, Sarah, Seth, Silas, Song, Sophie C., Sophie M., Tate, Teagan, Teddy, Theo, Wallace, Wiley, Zadie H., Zadie S., and Zora.

Lastly, I want to thank the team at Storey who helped me with this beautiful book, especially Jessica Armstrong, Lisa Hiley, and Deborah Balmuth, and our photographers, Julie Bidwell and Carl Tremblay.

Deanna Cook

CONTENTS

CHAPTER ONE

WELCOME TO COOKING CLASS!

CHAPTER TWO

BREAKFAST CAFÉ

CHAPTER THREE

LUNCH LESSONS

CHAPTER FOUR

SNACK ATTACK

CHAPTER FIVE
EAT YOUR VEGGIES

CHAPTER SIX
MY FIRST DINNERS

CHAPTER SEVEN
TIME FOR DESSERT

BONUS PULL-OUT FEATURES!

Stickers and Labels • Place Cards • Game Cards
• Recipe Cards

Fried Rice,
page 116

WELCOME TO COOKING CLASS!

Do you like to cook? Maybe you've helped your family in the kitchen with dinner or baked brownies for dessert with your friends. Or maybe you're just hungry for a homemade snack. This book is filled with lots of great recipes that teach kids how to cook. Each recipe was tested by kids just like you for ease ("Fast!" or "Took too long!"), taste ("Yum!" or "Yuck!"), and overall fun factor.

Before you put on your apron, take some time to read this introductory chapter all the way through. It has helpful tips for junior chefs, like what kitchen tools to have on hand and how to measure carefully. It also shows you how to properly use a paring knife and other ways to be safe in the kitchen. But most important, you'll learn how to cook up some fun in the kitchen!

Recipe Ratings

Each recipe is rated with one, two, or three spoons so you know the skill level needed to complete it. If you are a new chef, you can start with the easier recipes and work your way up.

ONE SPOON	**TWO SPOONS**	**THREE SPOONS**
You can cook most of these recipes without needing a hot stove or using a sharp knife.	You need to do some prep work, such as chopping or dicing. You'll also try out new kitchen skills. These are good recipes to work on with a parent or an older sibling.	These recipes involve cutting with sharp knives and using the oven and stovetop. They tend to take more time to prepare, too. If you are just learning to cook, work with an adult.

REVIEW THE RULES

Start good cooking habits from the get-go by following these basic kitchen rules. Ask an adult for permission to make a recipe. Ask for help, too, if you have questions along the way.

1 Wash your hands with warm water and soap before you handle food. Scrub well for 20 seconds, or as long as it takes to recite the alphabet.

2 Roll up very long or loose sleeves and wear an apron or smock (an oversize T-shirt will do the trick nicely). Tie back long hair to keep it away from food. You can even wear a bandanna or chef's hat!

3 Read the recipe from start to finish before you begin. Follow the steps closely.

4 Put out all the ingredients from the "Here's What You Need" list to be sure you have everything.

5 Measure carefully (see the tips in lesson 5).

6 Use a timer so you don't burn or overcook anything.

7 Always use pot holders when touching hot pans and dishes.

8 Most important, clean up afterward!

GET YOUR KITCHEN IN ORDER!

MAKE A RECIPE COLLECTION

Start with the recipes in this book—put a check mark next to each one you try. You can also create your own folder or recipe box for storing recipes from magazines and websites. Use the recipe cards in the back of the book to write down some favorite family recipes or ones that you come up with yourself.

CREATE A COOKING KIT

Find a box or clear plastic container and stock it with your own cooking tools. Label or decorate your container. (See the stickers in the back of the book.)

You'll want to start with:

- measuring spoons & cups
- whisk
- paring knife
- rolling pin
- clean scissors
- mixing spoon
- spatula
- tongs
- pastry brush
- melon baller
- pizza cutter

SET UP A GOOD WORK SPACE

- Clear off a kitchen countertop so you have plenty of room to cook. A kitchen table is a great place to prep food, too.

- If the work space is too high for you to comfortably reach, find a sturdy stool to stand on.

- Be sure the floor isn't wet—you don't want to slip and fall!

START WITH GOOD INGREDIENTS

MAKE A LIST before you shop. This will save you time and money, and you won't forget an important ingredient.

USE FRESH INGREDIENTS as much as possible. Whenever you can, choose organic fruits and veggies. They taste great, have more nutrients, and are better for the environment.

PICK YOUR OWN. If you're lucky enough to have a garden, you can pick veggies for your recipes. If not, stop at your nearest farmers' market to stock up. These markets usually also sell meats, cheeses, and eggs that are organic and/or local. During the winter, though, frozen vegetables often taste better and have more nutrients than fresh ones shipped from far away.

STORE YOUR PRODUCE properly until you use it, and clean it well before cooking. Rinse fruits and vegetables under cold water to remove any dirt. Use a scrub brush on hard items like carrots and potatoes to make washing them easier.

eggs
bread
milk
lettuce
carrots
strawberries
noodles

LESSON 4
KITCHEN VOCABULARY

Prep Work

Many of the recipes in this book call for prep work, such as grating carrots or crushing garlic, before you actually make the dish. Read the ingredient list to find out what you need to do. With all your prep work done in advance, you won't have to stop what you're doing as you cook. Here are some words you'll see in recipes.

BEAT. To mix rapidly with a wooden spoon, wire whisk, or electric mixer until smooth.

BLEND. A blender has very sharp blades that mix solid and liquid ingredients into a smooth paste or liquid. Be sure the top is on properly before you push the button!

CHOP. To cut food into pieces about 1-inch square. Chopped ingredients are often used in salads, soups, and stews.

CORE. To remove the stem and seeds from the middle of a piece of fruit with a knife or a special slicer or corer.

CRUSH. To smash an ingredient, often raw garlic, through a press or with the flat side of a knife. You can also use a rolling pin or even a can to crush nuts or seeds.

DICE. To cut food into pieces that are about ½-inch square. Strongly flavored ingredients like onions are often diced so they won't overwhelm the other flavors in the dish.

GRATE. To rub ingredients, such as cheese or carrots, against a grater to cut them into shreds. If the food gets too small, stop grating to protect your fingers. When you grate pieces of citrus, its called zesting (see page 167).

JUICE. To squeeze the juice from citrus fruit by cutting it in half and pressing the halves on a juicer. If you are juicing and zesting the same piece of fruit, it's easier to do the zesting first.

MINCE. To cut food, usually herbs and other flavoring ingredients, into tinier pieces than chopping or dicing. You can mince herbs with a small knife, but using scissors is easier.

MIX. To use a spoon or electric mixer to combine ingredients so they are evenly distributed. Use a mixing bowl that is big enough to hold everything with some extra space to avoid spills.

PEEL. Remove the skin from a fruit or vegetable by peeling it with a vegetable peeler. There are two kinds of peelers: a straight peeler and a Y-shape peeler (shown).

KITCHEN VOCABULARY

PREP WORK, *continued*

PROCESS. Some of the recipes in this book ask you to use a food processor. Read the manual or ask an adult for help the first time. Lock the top in place before you turn it on. Be extra careful when removing the blade for cleaning.

SLICE. To cut food into longer or thicker pieces. You can cut tortillas and other flat foods with a pizza cutter instead of a knife. Simply hold the pizza cutter firmly and roll it through the food in a straight line moving away from your body.

WHISK. Whisks come in many sizes for mixing dry or wet ingredients until they are well combined. Whisking works better with liquids; thick batters can get stuck in the wires.

Cooking Terms

Once all your prep work is done, you can start cooking! There's a whole vocabulary of cooking terms, too. Here are a few that you'll use in this book.

Warning: These skills involve using a hot stove or grill. Be extra careful around boiling water, hot oil, and open flames.

BAKE OR ROAST. Both of these terms mean to cook with dry heat in the oven, usually on an uncovered baking sheet or in a roasting pan. *Baking* is more often used with bread, cookies, and cakes, while *roasting* usually refers to meats and vegetables.

BOIL. To heat liquid at high temperature on the stovetop. When a liquid boils, bubbles rise rapidly to the surface. Always use a saucepan that is big enough to keep ingredients from boiling over the top.

FRY. This is a stovetop method of cooking food in an open pan in hot oil. Frying food can splatter the oil, so watch out.

GRILL. To cook food over a gas or charcoal fire outside.

MELT. To turn a solid into a liquid by applying low heat, such as melting butter in a saucepan or on a griddle, or melting chocolate chips in the microwave.

SAUTÉ. To cook food lightly in a little oil in a frying pan or skillet.

SIMMER. Turn the heat down to low to simmer liquids. The bubbles rise to the surface much more slowly than they do when the liquids are boiling.

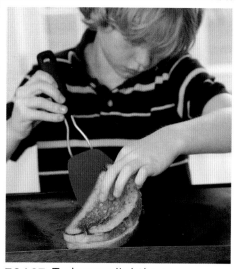

TOAST. To brown lightly on both sides. You can do this on a griddle or with a panini grill as well as a regular toaster.

EQUIVALENTS AND CONVERSIONS

Here's a handy chart to help you convert recipe measurements.

1 TEASPOON

= 5 milliliters

1 TABLESPOON

= 3 teaspoons
  (or ½ fluid ounce)

= 15 milliliters

¼ CUP

= 4 tablespoons

= 60 milliliters

½ CUP

= 4 ounces

= 120 milliliters

1 CUP

= 8 ounces

= 240 milliliters

1 PINT

= 2 cups

= 16 ounces

= 480 milliliters

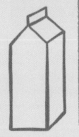

1 QUART

= 2 pints

= 0.95 liters

LESSON 5

MEASURE UP

When following a recipe, it's important to measure the ingredients carefully. Here are some tips:

LIQUID INGREDIENTS. Measure amounts of milk, water, and other liquids in a glass or plastic measuring cup. Pour the liquid into the cup and read the measure from eye level. For smaller measures, like a teaspoon, use measuring spoons.

DRY INGREDIENTS. It's important to measure flour, sugar, and other dry ingredients with dry measuring cups or measuring spoons that can be leveled off. Fill the cup or spoon with the ingredient, and then run the back of a butter knife across it to get an exact measure.

LESSON 6

CAREFUL WITH THE SHARP STUFF!

Many of the recipes in this book require that you use a knife, grater, food processor, or other sharp tools. It's easy to slip and cut your finger, so always work slowly and make sure your hands aren't wet and slippery.

KNIVES. All of the cutting can be done with a small paring knife (some soft foods can be cut with a plastic picnic knife or clean scissors instead). Make sure your paring knife is sharpened properly (dull knives are more dangerous because they can slip while you're cutting), and hold it firmly, with your fingers out of the way of the blade.

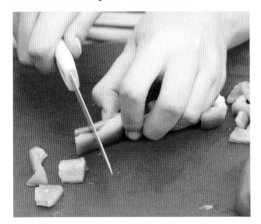

KITCHEN SCISSORS. A safer alternative to a sharp knife is a pair of scissors. Use kids' scissors instead super-sharp kitchen shears designed for adult hands. Keep a new pair in the kitchen for cooking projects.

GRATERS AND PEELERS. When you use a grater, whether for a chunk of cheese or a small carrot, watch out that you don't accidentally grate the tip of your finger or your knuckles. That can really hurt! The same goes for vegetable peelers, which can slip. Always push the blade away from your fingers, not toward them.

BLENDERS AND FOOD PROCESSORS. Be very careful when working with a blender or food processor, whether you are fitting the blades into the machine or taking them out to be washed. Never try to operate a blender or food processor with the lid off, and of course, never stick a spoon or spatula into the bowl without turning the machine completely off first.

COOKING WITH HEAT

Before you turn on the stove or oven, be sure to check first with an adult. They can show you the proper way to use the range and explain the different settings. When something is cooking on the stove, always stay in the kitchen!

Oven Safety

- Always use oven mitts or pot holders when handling hot pans and baking trays.

- When you open the oven, avoid the blast of heat that will rise up in your face.

Stovetop Safety

- Turn pan handles to the side so the pans don't accidentally get knocked off the stove.

- Be extra careful around boiling water and hot oil because steam and spattering fat can cause serious burns.

- Switch off the stovetop or oven when you have finished cooking.

Microwave Safety

- Different microwave ovens have different directions, so ask an adult to show you how to use yours.

- Never use metal or aluminum foil in the microwave. Always use microwave-safe dishes. Glass, paper towels, and most plastic containers are fine. If you aren't sure, ask an adult to show you which ones are safe. The wrong material could damage the microwave or even cause a fire.

- Be careful of escaping steam when lifting lids or plastic wrap from microwave dishes— it can burn you. If the microwave is located up high or over the stove, ask an adult to remove the hot dishes.

LET'S GET COOKIN'

LESSON 8
CLEAN UP

When you finish cooking, don't forget to leave the kitchen sparkling clean. Put away the ingredients, wipe down the countertop, and start the dishwasher. Here are some friendly reminders.

PUT AWAY ALL YOUR INGREDIENTS. It's especially important to return milk, meat, and other perishables to the refrigerator.

WIPE DOWN countertops and kitchen appliances with a wet sponge or kitchen washcloth.

LOAD THE DISHWASHER neatly with cups and dishes and start it when it's full.

WASH POTS AND PANS in hot, soapy water. Don't forget to scrub the handles and bottoms of the pots, too!

COMPOST nonmeat food scraps such as vegetable peels, watermelon rinds, and crumbled eggshells.

PICK A JOB, ANY JOB!

Nobody likes to clean up, but everyone should pitch in to get it done. A fun (and fair) way to divide up the chores is to make a jar full of job sticks.

Write each task on a clean ice-pop or craft stick. Put them in a jar and have everyone pick a job to do. That way no one gets stuck doing the same chore all the time. Here are some suggestions, but you can make the sticks fit your own household routine:

* Empty the dishwasher

* Load the dishwasher

* Wash pots and pans

* Dry pots and pans

* Wipe off the countertops and clean the sink

* Sweep the kitchen floor

* Take out the trash and/or recycling

My daughters, Ella and Maisie, always liked to include a "Free Card" stick so that the person who chose it could get off the hook for one job!

LESSON 9
TIME TO EAT!

One of the best things about cooking is sharing what you've made with family and friends.

START BY SETTING A NICE TABLE. The picture below shows where to put the silverware (forks go on the left and the knife and spoon on the right). Glasses should be placed just above the knife.

SPECIAL TOUCHES. It's fun to add a vase of fresh flowers as a centerpiece and make special place cards for everyone at the table (use the ones in the back of the book).

DON'T FORGET THE NAPKINS! Fold up some cloth napkins and set them on the table, too. You can find a fun way to fold them in the sidebar on the opposite page.

HOW TO . . .
FOLD A FANCY NAPKIN

FOLD OVER

Fold a napkin in half to make a triangle. Then fold over the two ends to make a square.

FOLD UNDER

Fold under one end of the napkin along the dotted line to make another triangle.

Bring the two ends toward each other to make a peak.

Now the napkin will stand on the table!

Bursting with Blueberries Muffins, page 40

BREAKFAST CAFÉ

Good morning! Ready to cook up the first meal of the day? In this chapter, you'll find easy and tasty recipes for eggs, granola bars, and even fancy French crêpes. You can pick some favorites and serve your parents breakfast in bed on Mother's Day and Father's Day. And how about cooking up some perfect pancakes with friends after a sleepover? So rise and shine and start cooking!

 SPOON

- My Own Cinnamon Sugar
- Freshly Squeezed Orange Juice
- Breakfast Sundaes

 SPOONS

- Mix-and-Match Fruit Flower Garden
- Have a Hard-Boiled Egg
- Grab-and-Go Granola Bars

SPOONS

- Ella's Egg Sandwich
- French Toast on a Stick
- Sleepover Party Pancakes
- Bursting with Blueberries Muffins
- Fancy French Breakfast Treats
- Simple Scones
- Crêpes with Nutella and Bananas
- Wallace's Omelet

MY OWN CINNAMON SUGAR

Makes ½ cup

Keep a jar of this sweet stuff in your kitchen. Sprinkle it on toast, oatmeal, and Cream of Wheat for a breakfast treat. It makes a great teacher gift, too!

Here's What You Need

½ cup sugar
2 tablespoons cinnamon

SPECIAL EQUIPMENT
Spice jar and label

HERE'S WHAT YOU DO

1 Measure the sugar and cinnamon into a bowl.

2 Use a spoon or mini whisk to mix them together.

3 Store in a spice jar with a label made by you.

FRESHLY SQUEEZED ORANGE JUICE

Makes 1 cup

Sure, you can quickly pour yourself a glass of orange juice from a carton. But with a few squeezes, you can make your own unprocessed OJ that tastes fresh from the tree.

Here's What You Need

1 or 2 oranges

SPECIAL EQUIPMENT
Manual juicer

HERE'S WHAT YOU DO

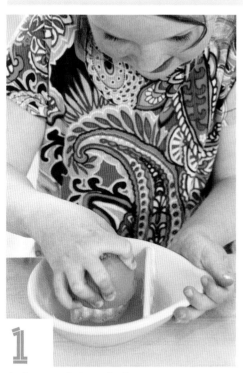

1

Ask an adult to help you cut the orange in half. Squeeze each half on a juicer. Twist it back and forth until all the juices are released.

2

Pick out the seeds. Pour the juice into a glass.

3

Drink it right up! It's fun to experiment with different kinds of oranges and even grapefruit.

OUR FAVORITE COMBOS

* **BANANA SPLIT:** Sliced banana, vanilla yogurt, cereal, and strawberries

* **BLUE CRUNCH:** Blueberry yogurt, blueberries, and granola

* **ALL-AMERICAN:** Vanilla yogurt, raspberries, blueberries, and puffed rice cereal

BREAKFAST SUNDAES

Makes 4 sundaes

Want to eat dessert for breakfast? Set up a sundae bar. It's a berry sweet way to start your day.

Here's What You Need

8	strawberries
1	banana
½	cup fresh blueberries or raspberries
2	cups yogurt
1	cup cereal, such as granola or whole-grain O-shapes

HERE'S WHAT YOU DO

1 Slice the strawberries into a bowl. Slice the banana into another bowl. Put the blueberries or raspberries in a third bowl.

2 Set out a bowl of yogurt and a bowl of dry cereal. Put a serving spoon by each bowl.

3 Then let everyone at the breakfast table dig in and build their own breakfast sundae with layers of yogurt, fruit, and cereal.

MIX-AND-MATCH FRUIT
FLOWER GARDEN

Plant fruit flowers on your breakfast table. Ask your friends to help, too. Together, you can make an edible flower garden—one with bugs and butterflies!

HAVE A HARD-BOILED EGG 🥄🥄

Makes 4 eggs

If you're hungry for a high-protein breakfast, boil up some eggs. Hard-boiled eggs are easy to make and fun to eat. You can do lots of things with them, from eating them right out of the shell to making egg salad sandwiches to creating cute critters to nibble on (see opposite page).

Here's What You Need

4   eggs (or as many as you want)
    Salt and black pepper

1 Place the eggs in a small saucepan and cover with cold water.

2 Bring the water to a boil over high heat. Boil for 1 minute, then turn off the heat. Put the lid on the saucepan and let the eggs sit in the hot water for 12 minutes.

3 Run the eggs under cold water to cool them off. Roll the eggs gently on all sides to crack the shells.

4 Peel off the shells. If it's hard to peel them, work under running water.

MAKE SOME EGG FRIENDS!

It's okay to play with your food when you're making art with it! You can have fun with hard-boiled eggs by turning them into animals and funny faces. Cut an egg in half or put slices of egg on crackers or Melba toast and decorate away.

Here are some suggestions for veggies to make eyes, ears, mouths, and even hair:

* Black and green olives
* Capers
* Small cherry tomatoes
* Carrot slices or slivers
* Green and red bell pepper slivers
* Chives, dill, parsley, and other herbs

* Pickle chips
* Radish slices
* Pickled beet slices or slivers

SILLY FACE

WISE OLD OWL

CAT BURGLAR

GRUMPY GUY

EGG MOUSE

TO MAKE EGG MICE, cut an egg in half lengthwise and place the halves on a plate. Cut tiny black olive eyes and slice thin radish or carrot rounds for ears. Make small slits in the egg for the eyes and ears. Push the olives and radishes into the slits. Add a chive tail and a carrot or olive nose.

GRAB-AND-GO GRANOLA BARS

Makes 12 bars

Looking for a quick breakfast you can eat on your way out the door? Mix up a batch of these chewy bars over the weekend. If you wrap them up individually and store them in the refrigerator, they'll stay fresh all week long.

Here's What You Need

- 3 tablespoons butter, plus more for the pan
- ⅓ cup packed light brown sugar
- ¼ cup honey
- 1 teaspoon vanilla extract
- 3 cups quick-cooking rolled oats
- ¼ cup chocolate chips

1 Butter an 8-inch square baking pan and set it aside. Melt the butter in a large pot over medium heat. Add the brown sugar, honey, and vanilla.

2 Whisk until the sugar is dissolved. Turn off the heat.

3 Pour the oats into the pot. Stir very well for about 5 minutes.

4

Spread the oat mixture into the pan. Press it into the pan with your hands to make it even (you may need to rub a little butter on your palms so they don't stick to the bars). Press hard!

5

Press the chocolate chips into the top of the bars. Cover with plastic wrap and refrigerate until chilled (about 1 hour).

6

Bring to room temperature, then ask an adult to help you cut it into 12 bars with a sharp knife. Wrap the bars individually in plastic wrap, aluminum foil, or waxed paper.

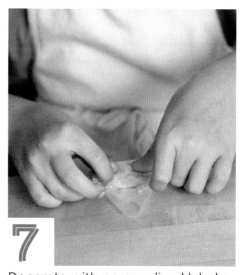

7

Decorate with personalized labels. Store in the refrigerator for up to 1 week.

CREATiVE COOKS!

GREAT GRANOLA

You can substitute ¼ cup of any of these mix-ins for the chocolate chips:

* Raisins

* Shredded dried coconut

* Dried cranberries

* Chopped dried apricots

* Mini M&M's

* Peanut butter chips

* Butterscotch chips

* Puffed rice cereal

Or try a combo with several of these mix-ins or any others that catch your fancy.

GRAB-
and-GO
GRANOLA
BAR

ELLA'S EGG SANDWICH

Makes 1 sandwich

On weekend mornings, my daughter Ella loves to cook up diner-style egg sandwiches. She uses Canadian bacon (you can find these round ham slices in most grocery stores). If she doesn't have that, she makes these sandwiches with sliced deli ham or bacon.

Here's What You Need

Butter, for the pan
1 egg
1 slice Canadian bacon
1–2 tablespoons grated or thinly sliced cheese (your favorite)
1 whole-wheat English muffin, toasted

HERE'S WHAT YOU DO

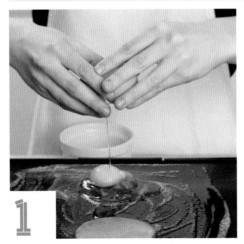

1 Melt a little butter in a griddle or skillet over medium-high heat. Crack the egg carefully onto the butter. Place a slice of Canadian bacon next to the egg.

2 Cook the egg until the white is mostly solid. Then flip it with a spatula. Flip the bacon over, too.

FOR SUNNY-SIDE UP, don't flip the egg.

FOR AN OVER-EASY EGG, cook for just a minute or two after you flip it, leaving the yolk a little runny.

FOR OVER-HARD, cook the yolk all the way through after you flip it.

3 Cover the egg with the cheese.

4 Cover the egg with a pan lid. Let the cheese melt and the egg finish cooking to your liking.

5 Place the egg and bacon onto the toasted English muffin. Eat right away or wrap it in aluminum foil to eat on the run.

HOW TO...
CRACK AN EGG

* Grab an egg and a small bowl. Whack the egg on the side of the bowl to make a crack. Try to whack it hard enough to crack the shell without smashing it. You don't want to wind up with a handful of crushed shell!

* Push your thumbs into the crack and pull the shell apart over the bowl.

* If you need a second egg, use another bowl. That way, if you mess up, you will get shells only in one egg, not two. If a piece of shell drops into the bowl, use one of the eggshell halves to scoop it out.

FRENCH TOAST ON A STICK

Makes 4 servings

Kebabs for breakfast? Sure! Just slide squares of French toast and fresh fruit onto wooden skewers for a fun start to the day!

Here's What You Need

- 3 eggs
- 1 cup milk
- 1 teaspoon cinnamon
- Butter, for the pan
- 1 small baguette, cut into 1-inch slices
- 10 strawberries
- 1 banana
- ½ cup blueberries
- Maple syrup or confectioners' sugar, for serving

SPECIAL EQUIPMENT
- Wooden or bamboo skewers

HERE'S WHAT YOU DO

1 Whisk the eggs in a pie plate or shallow bowl. Add the milk and cinnamon and whisk until it's all mixed together.

2 Heat a griddle or large skillet over medium heat. Melt a pat of butter in the pan and spread it around.

3 Dip both sides of each slice of bread into the egg mixture.

4 Add the slices to the pan and cook for 2 to 3 minutes, until light brown on the bottom. Flip each slice and cook the other side, then transfer to a cutting board.

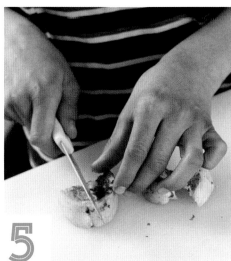

5

Cut the French toast into 1- to 2-inch squares. Cut the strawberries in half and slice the banana into ½-inch rounds.

6

Slide a piece of French toast, a strawberry half, a slice of banana, and a blueberry onto a skewer. Continue until the skewer is full. Repeat to make more kebabs.

7

Serve with maple syrup for dipping or confectioners' sugar for sprinkling.

SLEEPOVER PARTY!

When you and your friends wake up in the morning after a fun sleepover, move the party to the kitchen and make your own breakfast. Here are some recipes to try:

* Sleepover Party Pancakes (page 38)

* Freshly Squeezed Orange Juice (page 25)

* Breakfast Sundaes (page 26)

* French Toast on a Stick (page 34)

* Crêpes with Nutella and Bananas (page 46)

LET'S EAT!

MORE PLEASE!

HOW TO...
COOK BACON

Crazy for bacon? It's easy to cook some up for breakfast. Here are several methods—see which one works best for you.

In a microwave:

* Place four or five pieces of bacon between sheets of paper towel.

* Cook in the microwave on high power for 3 to 5 minutes, checking until the bacon is done the way you like it.

In a skillet:

* Heat the pan over medium heat.

* Add five or six bacon slices (don't crowd the pan too much).

* Cook on both sides until done, about 5 minutes per side, or longer for crispier bacon.

Watch for splattering grease with this method.

In the oven:

* Preheat the oven to 350°F (180°C).

* Arrange as many slices as you can in a single layer on an aluminum foil–lined baking pan.

* Bake until the bacon is crisp, 15 to 20 minutes.

PANCAKE PIZZAZZ

BLUEBERRY PANCAKES: Add a few blueberries to each pancake just after you pour the batter onto the griddle.

ANYTHING GOES: Add one or more of these: finely chopped apple or banana, shredded dried coconut, chopped walnuts, or even chocolate chips!

BIRTHDAY PANCAKES: For a special birthday treat, make your brother or sister a pancake in the shape of his or her age.

PERSONALIZED PANCAKES: Pour the batter into the shapes of the letters in your name.

SLEEPOVER PARTY PANCAKES

Makes 4 to 6 servings

Cook your pancakes on a large electric or stovetop griddle if you have one. That way, you can make a bunch of pancakes at once and none of your friends will have to wait! If you don't have a griddle, use a regular skillet. Keep the pancakes warm on a baking sheet in a 200°F (95°C) oven until you have enough for everyone.

Here's What You Need

1 cup flour
2 tablespoons sugar
2 teaspoons baking powder
   Pinch of salt
2 eggs

¾ cup milk
2 tablespoons butter, melted, plus more butter for the pan
   Maple syrup, for serving

1 Mix the flour, sugar, baking powder, and salt in a large bowl.

2 In another bowl, whisk the eggs. Then stir in the milk and melted butter.

3 Pour the egg mixture over the flour mixture and stir until mixed. It's okay to have a few lumps in the batter. If you mix it too much, your pancakes might turn out a little chewy.

4 Heat a griddle or skillet over medium-high heat. Melt a small pat of butter and spread it around with a spatula. Fill a ¼-cup measuring cup with pancake batter and ladle it on the griddle.

5 Repeat until the griddle is full, leaving a few inches between each pancake. Cook the pancakes until the edges are dry and bubbles appear on the surface, about 2 minutes.

6 Then flip and cook the second side. Serve the pancakes warm with maple syrup.

BURSTING WITH BLUEBERRIES MUFFINS

Makes 12 muffins

Packed with fresh blueberries, these sweet muffins are a nice morning surprise.

Preheat the oven to 375°F (190°C).

Here's What You Need

- 2 cups all-purpose flour (or 1 cup white and 1 cup whole-wheat flour)
- 2 teaspoons baking powder
- ½ teaspoon baking soda
- ¼ teaspoon salt
- ½ cup (1 stick) butter, softened
- 1 cup sugar
- 2 eggs
- 1 teaspoon vanilla extract
- ½ cup milk
- 2 cups blueberries

HERE'S WHAT YOU DO

1 Stir the flour, baking powder, baking soda, and salt in a medium bowl.

2 Cream the butter and sugar in a separate large bowl with an electric mixer until fluffy. Beat in the eggs, one at a time. Stir in the vanilla.

3 Mix in half the flour mixture, and then half the milk.

4

Add the rest of the flour and milk, and mix.

5

Add the blueberries to the batter, and use a rubber spatula to fold them in.

6

Line a 12-cup muffin pan with paper liners or grease the cups. Fill the muffin cups almost to the top with the batter.

7

Bake for 25 minutes, or until light brown.

CREATIVE COOKS!

STREUSEL TOPPING!

Add a little extra flavor and crunch to your blueberry muffins with a tasty topping.

In a bowl, mix together:

* 6 tablespoons flour

* 2½ tablespoons melted butter

* 1 tablespoon sugar

* 1 tablespoon brown sugar

* ⅛ teaspoon cinnamon

* ¼ teaspoon vanilla extract

You can do this with a fork or your clean hands. Sprinkle the streusel on top of the muffins before baking.

FANCY FRENCH BREAKFAST TREATS

Makes 12 muffins

It's fun (and tasty!) to dip these warm muffins into melted butter and roll them in cinnamon sugar.

Here's What You Need

MUFFINS
2	cups flour
¾	cup sugar
2	teaspoons baking powder
½	teaspoon salt
¼	teaspoon nutmeg
1	egg
1¼	cups milk
6	tablespoons butter, melted
1	teaspoon vanilla extract

TOPPING
⅔	cup sugar
1	teaspoon cinnamon
3	tablespoons butter, melted

Preheat the oven to 350°F (180°C).

1 Stir the flour, sugar, baking powder, salt, and nutmeg in a large bowl.

2 In a separate bowl, whisk the egg. Mix in the milk, melted butter, and vanilla.

3 Pour the egg mixture over the flour mixture, and stir until all the flour is mixed in.

4 Line a 12-cup muffin pan with paper liners or grease the cups. Spoon the batter into the muffin cups, filling each about two-thirds full. Bake the muffins for 20 minutes, or until light brown.

5 While the muffins cool slightly, mix the sugar and cinnamon in a small bowl. Pour the melted butter into a separate bowl.

6 Roll the warm muffin tops first in the melted butter and then in the cinnamon sugar.

SIMPLE SCONES

Makes 8 scones

Start your day with a traditional Scottish scone. Serve them warm with a little butter and a cup of fruit tea!

Here's What You Need

- 2 cups flour
- 3 tablespoons sugar
- 2 teaspoons baking powder
- ½ teaspoon salt
- ½ cup (1 stick) cold butter, cut into chunks
- 1 egg
- ½ cup milk
- ¼ cup raisins or currants

Preheat the oven to 425°F (220°C).

HERE'S WHAT YOU DO

1 Mix the flour, sugar, baking powder, and salt in a large bowl.

2 Use a pastry cutter or fork to cut the butter into the dough until it looks crumbly.

3 Whisk the egg and milk in a separate bowl. Pour the egg mixture over the flour mixture. Add the raisins and stir it up.

4 Dust your hands and a cutting board with flour. Knead the dough for a few minutes, and then pat it into a 7-inch circle.

5 Place the dough onto an ungreased cookie sheet. Cut it into 8 wedges with a pizza cutter or knife.

6 Separate the triangles so they are at least an inch apart. Bake for 15 to 18 minutes, or until golden.

Scones are best served warm!

CREATIVE COOKS!

SCONE STIR-INS

Instead of raisins or currants, try one of these combos or make up your own

* **CRANBERRY ORANGE:** Mix in ¼ cup dried cranberries and 1 teaspoon orange zest.

* **CHOCOLATE CHERRY:** Add ¼ cup chocolate chips and 2 tablespoons chopped dried cherries.

* **LEMON GINGER:** Add ¼ cup diced candied ginger and 2 teaspoons lemon zest.

* **CHEDDAR ROSEMARY:** Skip the sugar, and add ⅓ cup grated cheddar cheese and 1 teaspoon finely chopped rosemary.

Scones

CRÊPES WITH NUTELLA & BANANAS

Makes 4 servings

You can travel to France without ever leaving your kitchen! Just make these thin French pancakes and fill them with chocolate-hazelnut spread and bananas. Bon appétit!

Here's What You Need

- 1 cup flour
- 2 eggs
- 1¼ cups milk
- 2 tablespoons butter, melted, plus more butter for the pan
- 1 tablespoon sugar
- ¼ teaspoon salt
  Chocolate-hazelnut spread, such as Nutella
- 2 medium bananas, sliced

HERE'S WHAT YOU DO

1 Place the flour, eggs, milk, melted butter, sugar, and salt into a blender and blend until smooth.

2 Melt a little butter in a small skillet over medium heat and spread it around with a spatula. Pour about ¼ cup of the batter into the hot pan.

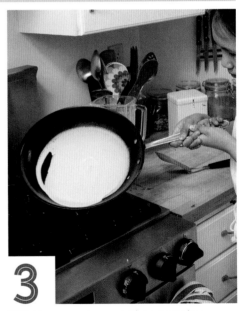

3 Tilt the pan to evenly coat the bottom.

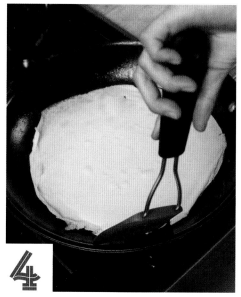

4 Cook for about 1 minute, then run a spatula around the edge of the crêpe.

5 Peek to see if it is lightly brown on the bottom. If so, flip the crêpe.

6 Cook on the other side until light brown. Transfer to a plate.

7 Spread with Nutella and banana slices. Fold into quarters, then dig in.

ALL KINDS OF CRÊPES

Crêpes are wonderfully versatile. Once you learn to make them, you can fill them with just about anything. Here are some ideas for both sweet and savory fillings.

* Sliced fresh fruit with yogurt or whipped cream

* Mixed berries, fresh or lightly cooked

* Jam or jelly with a sprinkle of crushed peanuts

* Fluffy scrambled eggs with chopped ham or bacon

* Shredded chicken and cheese

* Deli ham with Swiss cheese

* Deli turkey with chopped apples and dried cranberries

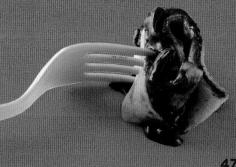

WALLACE'S OMELET

Makes 1 omelet

Wallace, who is 12 years old, says the best omelets start with the eggs he collects in his backyard chicken house. Try his secret for making omelets—add an extra egg yolk and a little grated butter—for a creamy, full flavor. (How do you grate butter? The trick is to freeze it first!)

Wallace likes to use a shallow cast-iron crêpe pan, but you can use any shallow pan with sloping sides.

Here's What You Need

- 2 eggs
- 1 egg yolk (see page 157 to learn how to separate eggs)
- 1½ teaspoons grated butter, plus 1 teaspoon butter
- 2 tablespoons grated cheese (your favorite)
- 2 fresh chives, snipped with scissors
  Salt and black pepper

SPECIAL EQUIPMENT
  Medium-size shallow pan
  Chopsticks

HERE'S WHAT YOU DO

1 Heat a skillet with sloping sides over medium heat. Whisk the eggs and the extra yolk in a bowl. Stir in the grated butter.

2 Melt the remaining 1 teaspoon butter in the hot pan. Pour in the eggs and cook for about 1 minute.

3 Poke holes in the egg mixture with the chopsticks. Then swirl the pan to fill the cracks.

4 Add the grated cheese and snipped chives.

5

Turn off the heat and cover the pan. Let the eggs cook for about 2 minutes longer.

6

Fold the omelet into thirds, like a letter, add salt and pepper to taste, and serve right away.

GOT CHICKENS?

Wallace and his sister, Audrey, have chickens in their backyard. Perhaps you have a flock of your own, or you know someone in your neighborhood who does. Fresh eggs from hens that are free to eat grass and bugs have really bright yellow yolks—compare them to regular grocery store eggs sometime!

49

Banh Mi Sandwiches, page 64

CHAPTER THREE

LUNCH LESSONS

It's lunchtime! Whether you are packing lunch for school or pulling together a hot lunch at home, preparing a midday meal is a great way to practice your cooking skills. In this chapter, you'll review the basics, like how to make peanut butter from real peanuts and how to cook up a mean grilled cheese sandwich. Once you have those recipes down, it's time to think outside of the lunch box and invent your own variations. That way, you'll never get stuck in a lunch rut.

SPOON

* Homemade Peanut Butter
* PB & Honey Pockets
* Lunch on a Stick

SPOONS

* Mix-and-Match Sandwich Shop
* Spinach Pinwheels
* Lettuce Roll-Ups
* Mix-and-Match Bento Boxes
* Banh Mi Sandwiches

SPOONS

* Toasty Melt
* Italian Panini
* Quiche Cupcakes

GO NUTS!

You don't have to stick to plain old PB&J sandwiches. Try one of these creative ways to use your homemade peanut butter.

* Peanut butter and bacon sandwich

* Peanut butter on banana slices

* Peanut butter on sliced apples

* Peanut butter on pretzel sticks

* Peanut sauce (see Think Spring Rolls, page 112)

* Peanut butter on pasta (see Nutty Noodles, page 128)

Kelly's HOMEMADE PEANUT BUTTER

Use a label from the back of the book or make your own.

HOMEMADE PEANUT BUTTER

Makes 2 cups

Have you ever seen whole peanuts transform into peanut butter? If not, give it a try and a taste test. Once you get the method down pat, you can experiment with other nuts, too. Almond butter, anyone?

Here's What You Need

2 cups salted roasted peanuts (shelled, of course!)
1 tablespoon vegetable oil
1 tablespoon honey

HERE'S WHAT YOU DO

1 Pour the peanuts and oil into the bowl of a food processor.

2 Process the peanuts for about 2 minutes. Then add the honey. Process until smooth, another minute or two.

3 Store in a jar in the refrigerator.

PB & HONEY POCKETS

Makes 2 pockets

Have you seen those crustless peanut butter sandwiches in the store? Instead of buying them, here's how to make your own healthier and tastier version at home.

Here's What You Need

- 2 slices soft sandwich bread
- 2–3 tablespoons peanut butter
- 2 tablespoons honey or jam

SPECIAL EQUIPMENT
Small round cookie cutter

HERE'S WHAT YOU DO

1 Roll one slice of the bread flat with a rolling pin.

2 Cut out two small circles with a round cookie cutter.

3 Spread a little peanut butter on one bread circle and top it with honey or jam. Don't go all the way to the edges.

4 Put the circles together to make a round sandwich. Using the tines of a fork, seal the sandwich pocket. Repeat the steps with the second slice of bread.

LUNCH ON A STICK

Makes 4 to 6 lunch sticks

If you're tired of boring old sandwiches for lunch, try this twist: Make a sandwich on a stick! You can cut a slice of meat into strips to fit on the toothpicks or, even easier, ask at the deli counter for a ½-inch-thick slice that you can cut into chunks. Mix and match to make your own favorite combos.

Made with my VERY OWN hands

Here's What You Need

¼–½ pound deli meat (ham, turkey, or salami), sliced
2 sticks string cheese or 6 small fresh mozzarella balls
2 large leaves red or green lettuce
2 slices bread, cut into 1-inch cubes
8 cherry tomatoes
Mayonnaise, ranch dressing, and mustard, for dipping

SPECIAL EQUIPMENT
Toothpicks

HERE'S WHAT YOU DO

1 Roll up the sliced meat and cut it into strips or cut it into chunks, depending on the thickness. Cut the string cheese into 1-inch pieces (you can leave the mozzarella balls whole or cut them in half). Tear the lettuce into small pieces.

2 Thread the toothpicks with the bread, meat, cheese, lettuce, and cherry tomatoes.

3 Make patterns or alternate colors! Serve with mayonnaise, ranch dressing, and mustard on the side for dipping.

COOL COMBOS

Try these sandwich stick combos.

* Fresh mozzarella, cherry tomatoes, and basil leaves

* Ham, cheese, lettuce, and bread

* Grapes and strawberries

* Lettuce, tomato, and cucumbers

MIX-AND-MATCH
SANDWICH SHOP

Get creative in the kitchen with these deli sandwich ideas. Check out these photos for inspiration or just let your taste buds tell you what to do. Pretend you own a deli and take orders from your "customers." (No doubt your parents, siblings, and friends would be happy to have you make them lunch!)

FUNNY FACE

Bagel + Carrot Stick Hair + Olive Eyes + Red & Yellow Bell Pepper Nose & Mouth + Cream Cheese

TURKEY CLUB

Toast + Turkey + Bacon + Lettuce + Tomato + Mayo

SUPER SUB

Sub Roll + Olive Oil + Salami +
Provolone + Lettuce + Tomato

SCARY SANDWICH

Wheat Bread + Cheese & Peas
Eyes + Bell Pepper Eyebrows
+ Sunflower Seed Teeth + Ham Tongue

TEA PARTY SANDWICHES

Thin White Bread + Mayo + Dill + Cucumbers

SPINACH PINWHEELS 🍴

Makes 8 to 10 servings

These spiral sandwiches, filled with flavored cream cheese and roasted red peppers, make a fancy lunch. Or serve a platter of pinwheels as finger food at your next party. They'll disappear fast!

Here's What You Need

- 1 garlic clove
- ½ (10-ounce) package frozen spinach, thawed and drained
- 1 (8-ounce) package cream cheese, softened
- ½ teaspoon salt
- ⅛ teaspoon black pepper
- 8 large flour tortillas, at room temperature
- 8 slices roasted red pepper

HERE'S WHAT YOU DO

1 Peel the garlic clove and place it in the bowl of a food processor. Process until it's finely chopped.

2 Set a colander in the sink and put the spinach in it. Press the spinach to remove as much liquid as possible.

3 Add the spinach and cream cheese to the food processor. Add the salt and black pepper, and process until creamy.

4 Place a tortilla on a piece of plastic wrap. Spread with some of the filling.

5 Add a slice of roasted red pepper. Roll up the tortilla into a log. Repeat with the remaining tortillas.

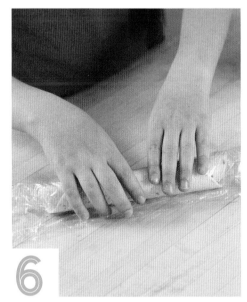

6 Wrap each log in the plastic wrap and refrigerate for at least 2 hours.

7 When you're ready to serve, slice the logs into 1-inch pinwheels and place on a plate with the spiral cut side up.

8 The ends don't make perfect pinwheels, so go ahead and eat them before serving up the rest to your guests!

LETTUCE ROLL-UPS

Makes 4 roll-ups

For lunch today, skip the bread and make a lettuce roll-up instead!

Here's What You Need

- 4   leaves lettuce
- 1–2 tablespoons mayonnaise or mustard
- 4   slices deli meat (ham, turkey, roast beef, or salami)
- 4   slices cheese

SPECIAL EQUIPMENT
Toothpicks

HERE'S WHAT YOU DO

1 Place a lettuce leaf on a cutting board. Carefully spread it with mayonnaise or mustard.

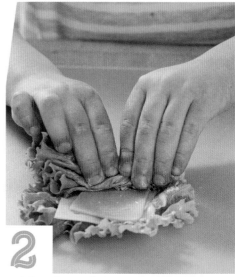

2 Add a slice of deli meat. Top with a slice of cheese.

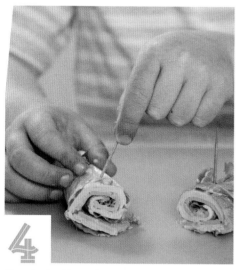

3 Roll up the leaf as shown.

4 Cut in half and push in a toothpick to hold it together! Repeat with the rest of the ingredients to make two more roll-ups.

PICNIC TIME!

Looking for something to do with your friends on a sunny day? Have a backyard picnic!

* Choose a sandwich in this chapter for your picnic fare.

* Follow the recipe and wrap the sandwich in foil or plastic.

* Grab a picnic basket and a blanket.

* Pack up your food, drinks, and napkins.

* Find a patch of grass in the backyard or a picnic spot in a park.

* Enjoy!

MIX-AND-MATCH
BENTO BOXES 🍴

Looking for an easy way to pack your own lunches? Start with a bento box and some leftovers from dinner! You can pick and choose proteins, vegetables, fruits, and side dishes for a personalized meal.

TEX-MEX

Soft Taco or Tortilla Chips + Salsa + Black Bean Salad + Cheddar or Jack Cheese + Star Fruit

MEDITERRANEAN FEAST

Hummus + Pita Chips + Carrots + Cucumber + Cherry Tomatoes + Stuffed Grape Leaves

THANKSGIVING TREAT

Turkey + Dried Cranberries + Potato Chips + Cherry Tomatoes + Green Beans + Pumpkin Muffin

ASIAN TAKE-OUT

Peanut Noodles
+ Orange Wedges +
Edamame + Bell Pepper
+ Rice Snacks

SPAGHETTI SUPPER

Leftover Spaghetti + Meatballs
+ Red Sauce + Bell Pepper + Olives
+ Shredded Mozzarella

BANH MI SANDWICHES

Makes 4 servings

Tired of your same old school lunch sandwich? Try this Vietnamese favorite made with pickled carrots and cucumbers, fresh mint and cilantro, and meat. The literal translation of *banh mi* is "bread," because the baguette is such an important part of this sandwich. Dig into one of the most delicious sandwiches in the world!

Here's What You Need

SANDWICH
- ½ cup white vinegar
- ½ cup sugar
- 1 cup grated carrots
- 1 cucumber, sliced into strips lengthwise
- ½ cup fresh cilantro leaves
- ½ cup fresh mint leaves
- 1 baguette, sliced lengthwise
- 8 slices cooked ham, cooked chicken, or tofu

SPICY MAYONNAISE
- 3 tablespoons mayonnaise
- 1½ teaspoons sriracha hot sauce

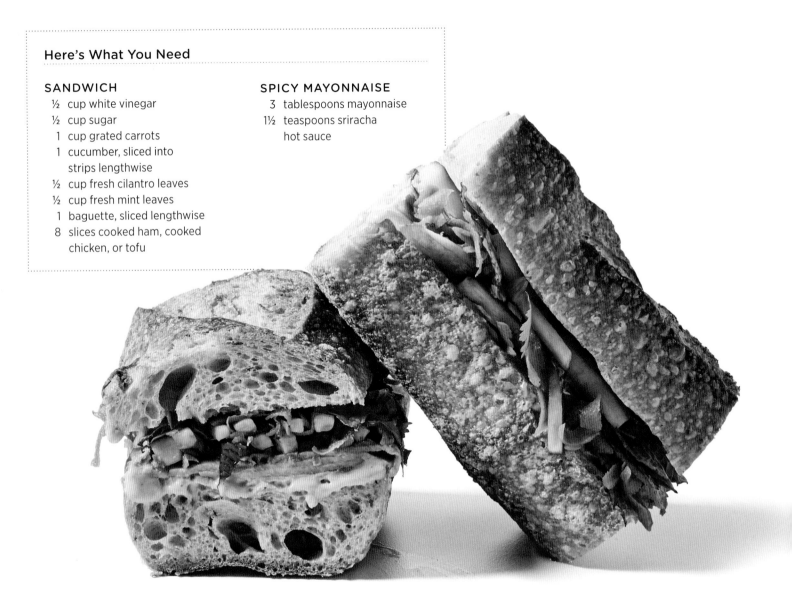

1 Mix the vinegar and sugar in a medium bowl. Add the grated carrots and cucumber slices. This is an easy way to "pickle" raw veggies. Let them pickle for 1 to 6 hours, then drain off the liquid.

2 Snip or chop the cilantro and mint and set aside.

3 Make the spicy mayonnaise: Mix the mayonnaise and sriracha sauce in a small bowl. Set aside.

4 Now you're ready to assemble the sandwich. Spread the spicy mayonnaise on the bread. Add a layer of ham, chicken, or tofu.

5 Top with the pickled carrots and cucumber slices. Sprinkle with the chopped cilantro and mint leaves.

6 Place the top half of the baguette on the sandwich. Slice into four portions for serving.

TASTY TOASTY COMBOS

Try these variations on melted cheese sandwiches.

* Sliced apples or pears and cheddar cheese

* Mozzarella, tomatoes, and pesto (see page 121 for a pesto recipe)

* Bacon, avocado, and Muenster cheese

* Cheddar, horseradish, and roast beef

* Ham, Swiss cheese, and Dijon mustard

TOASTY MELT

Makes 1 sandwich

On chilly or rainy weekends, it's fun to cook up a classic hot lunch. Here's a basic recipe for grilled cheese that you can jazz up with different cheeses, breads, and fillings (see Creative Cooks! for ideas).

Here's What You Need

2 slices bread
Butter, for the bread
1 or 2 slices cheese

HERE'S WHAT YOU DO

1 Heat a griddle or skillet over medium heat. Butter one side of a piece of bread and place it butter side down in the pan. Add the cheese. Butter the second slice of bread and place it butter side up on the sandwich.

2 Cook until the bottom slice is light brown and the cheese is melting, then flip the sandwich and cook on the other side until light brown. Slice in half and serve right away.

ITALIAN PANINI

Makes 1 panini

If you have a sandwich press, turn your kitchen into an Italian bistro and cook up a panini for lunch. This combo uses salami, mozzarella, and green bell pepper, but feel free to mix and match (see Creative Cooks! on opposite page).

Here's What You Need

2 slices bread
  Olive oil, for the bread
1 slice mozzarella cheese
1–3 slices salami
3 thin slices green bell pepper

SPECIAL EQUIPMENT
Sandwich press

HERE'S WHAT YOU DO

1

Have an adult show you how to plug in and warm up your sandwich press. You can read the manual, if you have it. Brush one side of each slice of bread with oil.

2

Place one slice, oil side down, in the sandwich press. Add the cheese, salami, and green bell pepper. Top with the second slice of bread, oil side up.

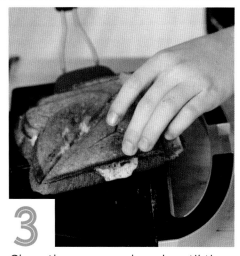

3

Close the press and cook until the cheese melts. (Some sandwich presses have a light that turns on when the sandwich is ready.)

QUICHE CUPCAKES

Makes 12 mini quiches

These yummy quiches are easy to prepare. Pack them in your lunch box with some veggies for a delicious, nutritious lunch.

Here's What You Need

- 3 eggs
- 3 tablespoons milk
- ¼ teaspoon salt
  Vegetable oil, for the muffin pan
- 2 tablespoons chopped cooked ham
- 1 tablespoon chopped tomato
- 1 tablespoon chopped green bell pepper or fresh spinach
- 2 fresh basil leaves, chopped
- ½ cup grated cheese (your favorite)

Preheat the oven to 350°F (180°C).

HERE'S WHAT YOU DO

1 Crack the eggs and whisk them together in a large measuring cup. Mix in the milk and salt.

2 Line the bottoms of a mini muffin pan with paper liners. Lightly spray or brush the bottom of the liners with oil to prevent the egg mixture from sticking.

3 Fill each cup with a bit of ham, tomato, green bell pepper or spinach, and basil.

4 Top with the grated cheese.

5 Pour the egg mixture over the fillings.

6 Bake in the oven for 10 to 12 minutes. Eat your quiche cupcakes warm or chill them to pack them in your lunch box.

LUNCH BOX EXTRAS

When you pack your lunch box, add some snacks, treats, and a pinch of fun. Here are some ideas.

* Cherry tomatoes or sliced carrots with Home on the Ranch Dressing (page 103)

* Pack a salad with your favorite dressing on the side (pages 102–103)

* Easy-Peasy Applesauce (page 86)

* Very Vanilla Pudding (page 156)

* Tortilla Chips from Scratch (page 91) and Gorgeous Garden Salsa (page 90)

* Berry Good Smoothie (page 72), packed in a thermos

* Minty Melon Bubbles (page 76)

Fruit Roll-Ups, page 94

CHAPTER FOUR

SNACK ATTACK

Hungry for an afternoon snack? Skip the store-bought chips and mix up your own snacks from scratch. In this chapter, you'll find yummy (and healthy!) recipes for homemade versions of your favorite packaged snacks. Try the fruit roll-ups or the chips and salsa. Making snacks can turn into a fun after-school activity. So when you step off the school bus and you're looking for something to do, head straight to the kitchen!

SPOON

* Berry Good Smoothies
* Yummy Yogurt Bark
* Minty Melon Bubbles
* Rainbow on a Stick
* My Own Microwave Popcorn
* Mix-and-Match Trail Mix

SPOONS

* Popcorn Balls
* We Love Biscuits!
* Easy-Peasy Applesauce
* Mean Green Guacamole
* Gorgeous Garden Salsa

SPOONS

* Tortilla Chips from Scratch
* Happy Hummus
* Fruit Roll-Ups
* Crispy Cheese Squares

BERRY GOOD SMOOTHIES

Makes 2 smoothies

For a quick, delicious snack, mix up your own smoothies. This recipe calls for frozen mixed berries (strawberries, blueberries, and raspberries) and fresh bananas. But you can substitute many other fruits: Try pineapple, mangoes, or acai berries.

Acai Berries

Pineapple

Here's What You Need

- ¾ cup frozen mixed berries
- 1 ripe banana, cut into 1-inch pieces
- 1 cup vanilla, strawberry, or blueberry yogurt
- 1 cup milk
  Whipped cream, optional

HERE'S WHAT YOU DO

1 Put the berries, banana, yogurt, and milk in a blender.

2 Put on the lid, then blend until smooth and purple. It may take a couple of rounds before all the fruit is ground up.

3 Pour into glasses, add a squirt of whipped cream, if using, and serve with a fancy straw.

Berry Good   Blueberry   Mango

SMOOTHIE STAND

On a hot day, skip the lemonade and sell smoothies instead!

* First, put a table in your front yard where an extension cord can easily reach (ask an adult for help).

* Make a colorful Smoothie Stand sign—and be sure to include the price you're charging for your smoothies.

* Gather cups and straws and a box for keeping the money.

* Put the smoothie ingredients in a cooler with ice.

* Plug in your blender.

* Post your sign and you're ready for business!

TIP: You can donate a portion of your sales to a charity of your choice. Love dogs? Write on your sign that you're raising money for your local animal shelter!

YUMMY YOGURT BARK

Makes 12 servings

Here's a frozen yogurt treat for a cooling-off snack on a hot day. You can try different fruits and toppings to change up the flavor. Use the suggestions or look in your kitchen cupboard for other ideas!

Here's What You Need

- 2½ cups vanilla yogurt
- 1 cup blueberries
- 1 cup strawberries, sliced into small pieces
- ½ cup crispy wheat cereal

HERE'S WHAT YOU DO

1 Line a baking sheet with parchment paper. Use a spatula or the back of a spoon to spread the yogurt evenly across the pan, at least ½ inch thick. If the layer is too thin, your bark won't set properly.

2 Press the blueberries, strawberry slices, and cereal into the yogurt. Cover up most of the white space.

3

Carefully place the baking sheet in the freezer. Freeze for 2 to 4 hours, or until the yogurt is completely frozen.

4

Remove the bark from the freezer. Slide the bark off the pan and break it into pieces with your hands or a knife. Store the pieces in the freezer in a plastic bag or container for up to a week.

MINTY MELON BUBBLES

Make 4 cups

You'll have a ball making this fresh fruit snack with a melon baller. If you don't have one of these handy kitchen tools, pick one up at a kitchen supply store or department store, or in the kitchen section of a large grocery store. Or you can cut up the melon into small chunks and call them Minty Melon Blocks instead!

Here's What You Need

1 cantaloupe
1 honeydew melon
½ small watermelon
5 sprigs fresh mint

SPECIAL EQUIPMENT
Melon baller

HERE'S WHAT YOU DO

1 Have an adult help you cut the melons in half. Using the melon baller, scoop out balls of the fruit into a large bowl until you have about 4 cups.

2 Wrap the leftover melon and store in the refrigerator.

3 Finely chop some mint leaves to get 2 to 4 tablespoons (depending on how minty you want the melon to taste). Stir the chopped mint into the melon balls.

4 Spoon the fruit into cups. Add an extra sprig of mint as a garnish.

RAINBOW ON A STICK

Makes 6 servings

Instead of ordinary fruit salad in a bowl, serve up a rainbow on a stick! This snack is fun to make and even more fun to eat, especially when dipped in a yummy lemon-honey-mint dipping sauce.

Here's What You Need

½ cantaloupe
6 fresh strawberries
18 fresh blueberries
12 green grapes
3 tablespoons honey

3 tablespoons lemon juice
Sprig of fresh mint

SPECIAL EQUIPMENT
Bamboo skewers (or toothpicks)

HERE'S WHAT YOU DO

1 Scoop the seeds out of the cantaloupe. Use a melon baller or cut slices of the melon into bite-size pieces.

2 Thread pieces of the fruit onto a skewer to create a rainbow. Start with a strawberry, then add a piece of cantaloupe, a couple of grapes, and a few blueberries. Repeat until each skewer is full.

3 Next, make the dipping sauce. Whisk the honey and lemon juice in a small bowl until well mixed. Snip a few leaves of mint into the mixture and stir to combine.

4 Pick up a stick and dip away!

MY OWN MICROWAVE POPCORN

Makes 1½ cups

Sure, it's easy to make store-bought microwave popcorn. But this all-natural version costs less, tastes better, and is much healthier. Give it a try!

Here's What You Need

- 3 tablespoons popcorn kernels
- 1 tablespoon butter
- ¼ teaspoon salt

SPECIAL EQUIPMENT
- Paper lunch bag

HERE'S WHAT YOU DO

1 Place the popcorn kernels in the paper bag. Fold over the top of the bag twice. Microwave for 2 to 3 minutes, or until the popping almost stops. Remove from the microwave.

2 Melt the butter in the microwave on medium power for 30 seconds. Open the bag and pour the butter over the popcorn. Add the salt, close the bag, and shake it all up. Serve right away!

MOVIE NIGHT

At your next sleepover party or family night, turn your living room into an at-home cinema complete with bags of homemade popcorn. Pick a good movie, get into your pj's, and dig in!

Pop Up Some Flavor!

If you're bored with plain old butter and salt, try these yummy variations instead. Just add the ingredients to your bag of popped corn and give it a good shake.

SAY CHEESE!: Drizzle 1 teaspoon olive oil over the popcorn. Add 1 tablespoon grated parmesan cheese and ¼ teaspoon salt.

TACO POPCORN: Mix 1 tablespoon melted butter with ½ teaspoon chili powder.

SUGAR AND SPICE: Mix 1 tablespoon melted butter with 2 teaspoons sugar and ½ teaspoon cinnamon.

PIZZA POPCORN: Mix 1 tablespoon melted butter with ½ teaspoon dried basil and ½ teaspoon dried oregano.

Conor's MICROWAVE POPCORN

YUM

MIX-AND-MATCH
TRAIL MIX

Whether you're hiking, skiing, or playing soccer, you'll need a high-energy snack to keep you going strong. Mix up your own GORP (which stands for Good Old Raisins and Peanuts), or try one of these variations. Just fill a snack cup or a ziplock bag with your mix and hit the trail.

Raisins + Pistachios + Granola + Sunflower Seeds

BIRD FOOD

JUST POPPIN' IN

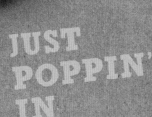

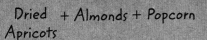
Dried Apricots + Almonds + Popcorn

SPORTS SWEETS

Raisins + Mini M&M's + O-Shaped Cereal

FALL FUN MIX

Dried Cranberries + Pumpkin Seeds + White Chocolate Chips

MONKEY MIX

Walnuts + Chocolate Chips + Dried Bananas

FOOD FUNDRAISER

Need an idea for your next school or sports team fundraiser? Set up a bake sale using recipes in this book. Wrap goodies up individually, add a price tag, and watch them fly off the table!

* Sell Popcorn Balls (this page) or bags of My Own Microwave Popcorn (page 78).

* Mix up a few batches of Grab-and-Go Granola Bars (page 30).

* Bake a batch of Little Lemon Squares (page 166).

* Serve up some of Maisie's Carrot Cupcakes (page 170).

* Bag up combos of Mix-and-Match Trail Mix (page 80).

* Make homemade candies from the Mix-and-Match Chocolate Factory (page 152).

POPCORN BALLS

Makes about 8 popcorn balls

Turn a batch of popcorn into popcorn balls for a sweet treat to share with friends.

Here's What You Need

4 tablespoons butter, plus a little more for your hands

1 (10-ounce) package mini marshmallows

7 cups popped popcorn (about ¼ cup kernels)—see popping instructions on page 78

sweet!

CHRIS's · BALL of · YUM!

HERE'S WHAT YOU DO

1 Melt the butter in a large saucepan over medium-low heat.

2 Add the marshmallows to the pan and stir until they're completely melted. Turn off the heat.

3 Pour the popcorn into the pot and stir well to coat all the kernels.

4 When the popcorn mixture is cool enough to handle, rub a little butter on your hands, grab a handful of the mixture, and gently pat it into a ball.

5 Set the ball on a plate and repeat with the remaining popcorn until it's all used.

6 Eat right away!

To save them for later, let the balls cool completely, then wrap each one in plastic wrap.

WE LOVE BISCUITS!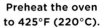

Makes 10 to 12 biscuits

Biscuit dough is a little like Play-Doh. You can shape it, roll it, and cut it into stars and hearts.

Here's What You Need

- 2 cups flour
- 1 tablespoon baking powder
- 1 tablespoon sugar
- 1 teaspoon salt
- 5 tablespoons cold butter
- ¾ cup milk

Preheat the oven to 425°F (220°C).

1 Whisk the flour, baking powder, sugar, and salt in a large bowl. Cut the butter into small chunks. Use a pastry cutter or fork to mix the butter into the dry ingredients until the dough is crumbly.

2 Pour in the milk. Stir until it forms a rough ball. You can switch to mixing with your (clean!) hands if it's too hard to stir. The dough will be a little bit sticky, so dip your hands in flour first.

3 Transfer the dough to a countertop dusted with flour. Knead the dough a few times, then shape it into a large ball.

4 Roll or pat the dough into a flat circle about ½ inch thick (the biscuits will double in thickness as they bake).

5 Dip a cookie cutter in flour and use it to cut out the biscuits. Place them a few inches apart on an ungreased or parchment-lined baking sheet. Bake the biscuits for 12 minutes, or until lightly browned.

EASY-PEASY APPLESAUCE 🥄🥄

Makes about 5 cups

Sure, you've eaten plenty of applesauce, but have you ever tried cooking it from freshly picked apples? All you need is a pile of apples and a little patience while they cook.

Here's What You Need

12 medium apples	Juice from	2 teaspoons
1 cup apple cider	½ lemon	cinnamon,
or water	½ cup sugar	optional

HERE'S WHAT YOU DO

1 Peel, quarter, and core the apples. Chop the quarters into chunks and place them in a large pot. Add the cider or water, lemon juice, sugar, and cinnamon, if using.

2 Cook the apples over medium heat until they are soft, 15 to 20 minutes. Stir well with a large spoon or a potato masher to mash up the apples.

3 Cool the applesauce before spooning it into small jars with lids. Store in the refrigerator for up to 2 weeks.

PICK YOUR OWN

For the freshest, tastiest apples, pick your own right off the tree. Bring an apple picking bag or basket along with you.

As you pick, don't tug the apples to pull them off the tree. Instead, lift up and gently twist the stem to remove the apple from the branch.

Gala

Fuji

Cripps Pink

McIntosh

Honeycrisp

Envy

Granny Smith

GUACAMOLE STIR-INS

Add a little zesty flavor to your guacamole with one or more of these additions:

* 2 tablespoons salsa

* ½ garlic clove, crushed

* 2 tablespoons grated Monterey Jack cheese

* 1 tablespoon finely diced onion

* 1 tablespoon chopped fresh cilantro

MEAN GREEN GUACAMOLE

Makes 1½ cups

Smooth, creamy guacamole is easy to make. Just add homemade chips and salsa and invite your friends to a Mexican fiesta!

Here's What You Need

- 2 ripe avocados
- ½ lime
- ½ teaspoon salt
  Optional ingredients
  (see Creative Cooks!)

HERE'S WHAT YOU DO

1 Cut the avocados in half and remove the pits (see opposite page). Scoop the flesh into a medium bowl and mash it with a fork or potato masher.

2 Squeeze in the lime juice. Add the salt and any optional ingredients. Stir it all up.

3 Taste the guacamole. Add more salt or lime juice, if you like. Serve right away with chips!

CUT AN AVOCADO

1 Start with a ripe avocado. It should feel soft but not too mushy. Cut the avocado in half with a sharp knife, working around the pit (ask an adult for help).

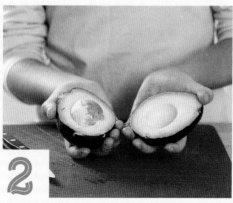

2 Twist the cut avocado into two halves.

3 Pop out the pit with a spoon.

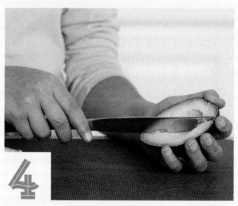

4 Hold one avocado half, cut side up, in the palm of your hand. Using a butter knife, cut long lines down the avocado.

5 Next, cut lines across the avocado, as shown.

6 Scoop out the diced avocado pieces with a spoon into a bowl.

HERE'S A COOL TIP FOR STORING GUACAMOLE, assuming it isn't all eaten! Keep one of the pits and push it into the container before putting the lid on. The guacamole will stay bright green.

GORGEOUS GARDEN SALSA 🍴🍴

Makes 1 cup

When tomatoes are ready to pick in the garden, try making your own salsa from scratch. This salsa calls for mild chile pepper, but you can use a hotter type if you like more spice or a green bell pepper for a nonspicy version. However you make it, it tastes great scooped up on homemade tortilla chips (see opposite page).

BE CAREFUL: The oil from chile peppers can burn, especially if you get it on your skin or touch your eyes. Wear rubber gloves, if you have them. Or just use caution.

When you cut open the chile, scrape away the seeds before you chop it up. After you finish, wash your hands well with soap!

Here's What You Need

- 1 large tomato
- ½ garlic clove
- 1 mild green chile pepper
- 5 sprigs fresh cilantro
- ¼ lime
- Salt
- Tortilla chips, for serving

HERE'S WHAT YOU DO

1 Dice the tomato and put it into a medium bowl. Crush the garlic and add it to the tomato. Mince the chile pepper and add 1 tablespoon to the salsa (you can add more after you taste it in step 4).

2 Finely chop the cilantro. Measure out 2 tablespoons and stir it into the salsa.

3 Squeeze the juice from the lime quarter over the salsa. Add a pinch of salt and stir again.

4 Taste the salsa and add more salt, lime juice, garlic, or chile pepper, if you like.

TORTILLA CHIPS FROM SCRATCH

Makes 4 servings

When you run out of tortilla chips, it's easy to make them from real tortillas. Cut the tortillas with a pizza cutter, then fry them up in your own private tortilla chip factory.

Here's What You Need

4–6 corn tortillas
1–2 tablespoons vegetable oil
Salt

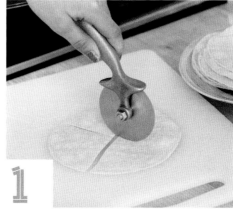

1

Cut the tortillas into triangles with a knife or a pizza cutter. Line a platter with paper towels and set aside.

2

Heat the oil in a skillet over medium-high heat. Fry the tortillas for about 1 minute, or until light brown. Watch closely, because they cook fast! Use tongs to carefully flip them over and cook the other side.

3

Place the chips on paper towels. Sprinkle with salt and serve right away.

HAPPY HUMMUS 🥄🥄🥄

Makes 6 to 8 servings

Skip the store-bought hummus and try making from scratch this tasty chickpea spread that's popular throughout the Middle East and beyond. Serve it with pita chips and cut-up veggies for a healthy snack.

Here's What You Need

- 1 (15-ounce) can chickpeas
- 1 garlic clove
- ½ teaspoon salt
- 3 tablespoons tahini paste
- 2 tablespoons lemon juice (about ½ lemon)
- 1 tablespoon olive oil, plus more olive oil for drizzling
  Toppings of your choice, optional

HERE'S WHAT YOU DO

1 Drain the canned chickpeas, saving the liquid in a measuring cup.

2 Peel the garlic clove and place it into a food processor. Process until it's finely minced.

3

Add the chickpeas, salt, tahini, lemon juice, and oil to the food processor. Purée the mixture.

4

Turn off the food processor and add 1 tablespoon of the reserved liquid from the chickpeas. Purée until the consistency is nice and creamy.

5

You can add up to 2 more tablespoons of the chickpea liquid if you want your hummus extra creamy. The hummus will thicken in the refrigerator.

6

Transfer the hummus to a bowl. If you like, sprinkle with any of the toppings listed at right, or drizzle with a little more oil. Store in the refrigerator.

TOP THIS!

Sprinkle a pinch of extra flavor on your hummus.

CUMIN

POMEGRANATE SEEDS

PINE NUTS

PAPRIKA

CHOPPED PARSLEY

FRUIT ROLL-UPS 🥄🥄🥄

Makes 12 to 14 pieces

You can make your very own fruit leather with almost any kind of fruit (this recipe uses mixed berries). It takes just a few minutes to mix up the fruit, but several hours to dry it in the oven. So plan to make these on a day when you're hanging around the house.

Preheat the oven to 200°F (95°C).

Here's What You Need

3 cups fresh mixed berries
2 tablespoons honey

HERE'S WHAT YOU DO

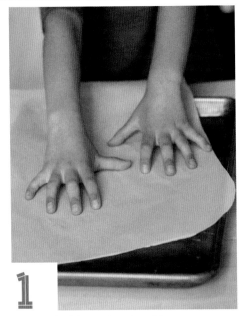

1 Line a baking sheet with parchment paper and set aside.

2 Pour the berries into the bowl of a food processor.

3 Add the honey and process until smooth.

4

Pour the fruit over the parchment paper. Evenly spread with the back of a spoon into a thin, large rectangle. Don't leave any super-thin areas or the leather will crack!

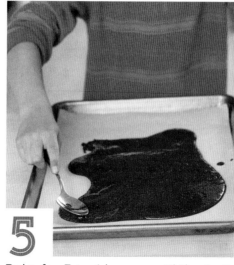

5

Bake for 3 to 4 hours, until the fruit feels dry and no longer sticky. Let cool for 2 to 3 hours, until it softens up enough to bend.

6

Peel the fruit leather off the parchment paper and transfer to a cutting board. Cut with a pizza cutter into strips.

7

To store, wrap each ribbon in a strip of plastic wrap, then roll it up.

FRUIT 'STACHES

Turn your fruit roll-ups into fun shapes simply by cutting them with kitchen scissors. August, Conor, and Chris made mustaches, eyebrows, and even a goatee!

CRISPY CHEESE SQUARES

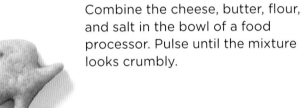

Makes about 2 dozen squares

If you're a fan of cheese-flavored crackers, try making them from scratch with real shredded cheese. You may never eat them from a box again!

Preheat the oven to 350°F (180°C).

Here's What You Need

- 2 cups (8 ounces) shredded cheddar cheese
- 4 tablespoons butter, cut into chunks
- 1 cup flour
- ¼ teaspoon salt
- 3 tablespoons milk

HERE'S WHAT YOU DO

1

Combine the cheese, butter, flour, and salt in the bowl of a food processor. Pulse until the mixture looks crumbly.

2

Pour the milk through the top of the food processor. Pulse until the dough starts to stick together.

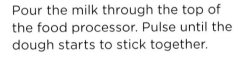

96

3

Remove the dough from the bowl, gathering the crumbs together into two balls.

4

Flatten the balls into disks between sheets of plastic wrap. Wrap them up, and refrigerate for at least 10 minutes (or up to 3 days).

5

Roll the dough to ¼-inch thickness. (If it's too hard to roll, let it soften on the counter for a few minutes.)

6

Cut the dough into 1-inch squares with a knife or a pastry or pizza cutter (or cut it into shapes with a small cookie cutter).

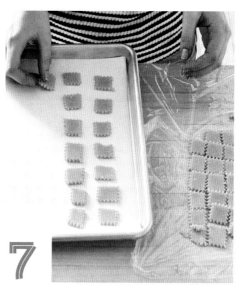

7

Place the crackers on a baking sheet lined with parchment paper.

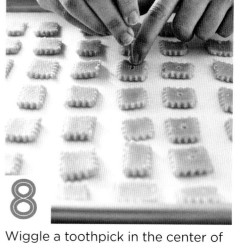

8

Wiggle a toothpick in the center of each square to make a hole. Bake for 8 to 12 minutes, or until crispy. Cool on the pan for a few minutes before eating them.

Tiny Tomato Toasts,
page 106

CHAPTER FIVE

EAT YOUR VEGGIES

How many times have you heard "Eat your veggies!" But how many times have you actually cooked up a veggie recipe on your own? When you chop, stir, and prepare salads and other foods made with fresh vegetables, you'll grow to love everything green—and red and orange and yellow. . . . Veggies are not only colorful and nutritious, they also have all kinds of interesting tastes, so you're sure to find some that you like. In this chapter, you'll learn how to make restaurant-style salads, roasted roots, and more veggie dishes that you—and your family—will eat up.

 SPOON

* Veggie World
* Salad Dressing Factory

 SPOONS

* Mix-and-Match Salad Bar
* Tiny Tomato Toasts

 SPOONS

* Roasted Roots
* Think Spring Rolls
* Iris's Corn & Black Bean Salad
* Fried Rice

VEGGIE WORLD

Go ahead and play with your food! Gather a bunch of fresh veggies (carrots, broccoli, bell peppers, cauliflower, summer squash, whatever you like), a paring knife, and a large platter or cutting board. Then start designing your own landscape with broccoli trees, cauliflower clouds, and carrot flowers. Serve the Veggie World with homemade dressing for dipping. Be creative with your designs—the sky's the limit!

SALAD DRESSING FACTORY

Making your own salad dressing is a snap. You just have to measure all the ingredients carefully and stir or shake it up well. Store it in a jar or bottle with a label you've designed yourself or one from the back of the book.

Then toss your dressing with salads or use it as a dip for veggies.

Here's What You Need

- ½ cup vegetable oil
- ¼ cup maple syrup
- ¼ cup cider vinegar
- 2 teaspoons Dijon mustard
- 1 garlic clove, crushed
  Salt and black pepper

HERE'S WHAT YOU DO

1 Combine the oil, maple syrup, vinegar, mustard, and garlic in a small jar with a lid.

2 Tighten the lid and shake it all up. Add salt and pepper to taste.

3 Serve it right away, or store in the refrigerator. Serve at room temperature.

Makes 1 cup

Here's What You Need

- ½ cup sour cream
- ¼ cup mayonnaise
- 2–3 tablespoons milk
- 1 tablespoon fresh-squeezed lemon juice
- ¼ cup crumbled Gorgonzola cheese (or any blue cheese you like)
  Salt and black pepper

HERE'S WHAT YOU DO

1 Mix the sour cream, mayonnaise, milk, and lemon juice in a small bowl until creamy and smooth.

2 Stir in the Gorgonzola and add salt and pepper to taste. Serve it right away, or store in a jar in the refrigerator.

Makes 1 cup

Here's What You Need

- 1 cup olive oil
- ⅓ cup balsamic vinegar
- 1 garlic clove, crushed
- ½ teaspoon dried herbs (such as basil, tarragon, or thyme) Salt and black pepper

Here's What You Need

- 1 cup olive oil
- ⅓ cup fresh-squeezed lemon juice
- ½ cup grated parmesan cheese
- 1 garlic clove, crushed Salt and black pepper

Here's What You Need

- ½ cup sour cream
- ½ cup mayonnaise
- 2–3 tablespoons milk
- 1 teaspoon white vinegar
- 1 sprig fresh flat-leaf parsley
- 1 sprig fresh dill
- ½ garlic clove, crushed Salt and black pepper

HERE'S WHAT YOU DO

1 Combine the oil, vinegar, garlic, and herbs in a small jar with a lid.

2 Tighten the lid and shake it all up. Add salt and pepper to taste.

3 Serve it right away, or store in the refrigerator. Serve at room temperature.

Makes 1⅓ cups

HERE'S WHAT YOU DO

1 Combine the oil, lemon juice, parmesan, and garlic in a small jar with a lid.

2 Tighten the lid and shake it all up. Add salt and pepper to taste.

3 Serve it right away, or store in the refrigerator. Serve at room temperature.

Makes 1½ cups

HERE'S WHAT YOU DO

1 Stir together the sour cream, mayonnaise, milk, and vinegar in a small bowl.

2 Snip the parsley and dill into tiny pieces with clean scissors. Measure about 1 tablespoon of each into the bowl.

3 Add the garlic, and salt and pepper to taste, and stir. Give it a taste test, and add more salt or herbs, if you like. Serve it right away, or store in a jar in the refrigerator.

Makes 1 cup

MIX-AND-MATCH
SALAD BAR

Do you like restaurant salad bars? If so, set up your own at home on your kitchen table and invite friends and family to dig in. Anything goes: salad greens, tomatoes, berries and other fruit, smoked turkey or ham, even nuts. Put everything in individual serving bowls. Now hand out plates and watch the salad chefs in action. Here are some combos to chew on:

GREEK

Romaine Lettuce + Cucumbers + Tomatoes + Olives + Feta Cheese + Balsamic Vinaigrette

WALDORF

Oak Leaf Lettuce + Blue Cheese + Apples + Walnuts + Balsamic Vinaigrette

GARDEN

Ranch Dressing
+ Mesclun Greens
+ Tomatoes + Grated
Carrot + Mushrooms
+ Chives

COBB

Bibb Lettuce + Cheddar Cheese + Bacon
+ Hard-Boiled Eggs + Turkey + Tomatoes

STRAWBERRY SPINACH

Spinach + Strawberries + Sliced
Almonds + Maple-Mustard Dressing

105

TINY TOMATO TOASTS

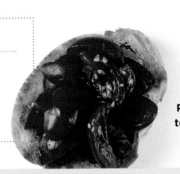

Makes about 2 dozen toasts

This appetizer, also known as bruschetta, is made of toasted bread that's topped with tomatoes. Bruschetta comes from the Italian *bruscare*, meaning "to roast over coals." This refers to the bread, not the toppings. It's a tasty snack anytime and fancy enough for a party.

Here's What You Need

12 cherry tomatoes	6 basil leaves, chopped
1 garlic clove, crushed	Salt and black pepper
3 tablespoons olive oil	1 baguette
1 teaspoon balsamic vinegar	

Preheat the oven to 350°F (180°C).

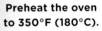

HERE'S WHAT YOU DO

1 To make the tomato topping, cut the tomatoes into quarters and put them in a bowl.

2 Add the garlic, 1 tablespoon of the oil, the vinegar, and the basil. Stir well, then add salt and pepper to taste. Set aside.

3 Ask a grown-up to help you slice the baguette into ½-inch slices and arrange them on a baking sheet. Measure the remaining 2 tablespoons oil into a small bowl. Add a pinch of salt. Paint the oil on both sides of the bread with a pastry brush.

106

4

Bake until the bread is lightly toasted, about 7 minutes per side. Use tongs to turn the bread over once during baking. Put the toasts on a serving platter and spoon the topping onto each toast just before serving.

Or you can place the tomato topping in a bowl with a spoon so people can serve themselves.

MORE TINY TOAST TOPPINGS!

Not a fan of tomatoes? Try any of these other toppings on your toast:

CUCUMBER DREAM

Cream Cheese + Cucumber Slice + Chopped Mint

MEXICAN MUNCH

Avocado Slice + Diced Red Bell Pepper + Squeeze of Lime Juice

FRENCH FAVORITE

Butter + Radish Slice + Chopped Chives

SWEET SNACK

Honey + Apple or Pear Slices + Crumbled Blue Cheese

HERE WE GROW!

Do you have a garden at your home or school? If so, offer to help water, weed, and pick fresh veggies for the recipes in this book. (This is Maisie's backyard garden, and she's picking with Adia and Theo.)

If you don't have a garden, talk to your parents or your teacher about starting one. Digging and planting in the soil are fun, and gardening is a great way to grow to love fresh veggies, fruits, and herbs. Garden foods taste yummy in recipes, plus they'll inspire some cooking creations in the kitchen.

For more information on how to get growing, contact Edibleschoolyard .org or Kidsgardening.org.

GIVE VEGGIES A BATH!

Are your beets, carrots, potatoes, and lettuces covered in dirt? After you dig them from the garden or buy them at a farmers' market, brush off any loose dirt before you bring them into the house. Then head straight to the kitchen sink for bath time!

TOMATOES, PEPPERS, CUCUMBERS, AND THE LIKE. Put garden-fresh veggies into a colander set in the sink. Rinse them with running water—a spray attachment is handy, if you have one.

ROOT VEGGIES (SUCH AS BEETS, POTATOES, AND CARROTS). Grab a vegetable scrub brush, turn on the faucet, and scrub away. Don't be afraid to scrub hard! You'll want to peel carrots, beets, and some other (but not all!) root veggies before you use them in recipes.

LETTUCE, SPINACH, KALE, AND OTHER LEAFY GREENS. Remove the outer leaves from head lettuce and tear the rest into bite-size pieces. You may need to swish lettuce and spinach leaves around in a bowl of water to loosen the dirt before using a salad spinner to get rid of the water. Run large leaves like kale and chard under the faucet, making sure to rinse all the crinkles.

CREATIVE COOKS!

BEETS? YUCK!

Don't like beets? You might change your mind after you try them roasted in this recipe. Or you can skip the beets and choose one of these suggestions instead. Just be sure to cut everything into chunks of about the same size, so they all cook evenly.

BEETS

TURNIP

CAULIFLOWER

SWEET POTATO

PARSNIP

CABBAGE

RED BELL PEPPER

POTATOES

CARROTS

LEEK

BRUSSELS SPROUTS

JUST ONE BITE! Don't be afraid to try a new veggie. To be a good cook, you have to learn the flavors of lots of different ingredients. Start your food adventure by tasting just one bite of as many veggies as you can. The more foods you try, the better a chef you'll be.

And if you don't like something at first, try it again in a few months. You might be surprised at how your tastes change.

110

ROASTED ROOTS 🥄🥄🥄

Makes 4 to 6 servings

Roasting, or baking in a hot oven, is one of the easiest ways to cook veggies, and it makes them extra delicious. You can roast just about any kind of vegetable. This recipe calls for root veggies like beets, and potatoes, which grow underground. Add or subtract vegetables from the ingredient list as you like. (Tip: For homemade tater tots, cook just the potatoes and garlic.)

Here's What You Need

3 medium potatoes	3 garlic cloves
2 medium beets	2–3 tablespoons olive oil
1 green or red bell pepper	1 teaspoon salt
1 medium onion	

Preheat the oven to 425°F (220°C).

HERE'S WHAT YOU DO

1

Peel the potatoes and beets. Cut the potatoes, beets, bell pepper, and onion into 1-inch chunks. Thinly slice the garlic.

2

Place all the veggies on a large baking sheet. Drizzle with the oil and sprinkle with the salt.

3

Toss with your (clean!) hands. Arrange in a single layer. Roast the veggies for about 45 minutes, until lightly browned and soft inside. Stir them every 15 minutes or so with tongs or a spatula.

THINK SPRING ROLLS 🥄🥄🥄

Makes 6 to 8 servings

For a no-cook dinner on a hot night, try this Vietnamese favorite. Fill papery rice rounds with lettuce, grated carrot, and fresh herbs. (You can buy the rounds in the international section of most grocery stores.) Roll them up, step back, and watch them disappear!

Here's What You Need

- 1 head Boston lettuce, chopped
- 2 carrots, grated
- 10 sprigs fresh mint, finely chopped
- 10 sprigs fresh cilantro, finely chopped
- 1 cup chopped cooked shrimp, tofu, chicken, or pork
- 12 spring roll wrappers
- 2–3 tablespoons hoisin sauce
- ¼–½ cup chopped peanuts, optional
- Dipping sauce, for serving (recipe on opposite page)

HERE'S WHAT YOU DO

1 Lay out the lettuce, carrots, mint, cilantro, and shrimp or other protein on a large plate or cutting board.

2 Fill a pie plate with warm tap water. Soak one spring roll wrapper until soft, about 30 seconds.

3 Working with the rice paper wrappers can be a little tricky (and sticky!) at first, but with a some practice, you'll soon get the hang of it. It's cool to see the sheets transform from crisp wafers to slippery wrappers!

4 To assemble a roll, place the softened wrapper on a cutting board and top with the lettuce, carrots, mint, cilantro, and shrimp or other protein. Add a teaspoonful or so of hoisin sauce and sprinkle with some peanuts, if you like.

DIPPING SAUCE

Makes about ¾ cup

Here's What You Need

¼ cup smooth peanut butter
¼ cup hot water
2 tablespoons soy sauce
2 tablespoons honey
2 tablespoons fresh-squeezed lime juice

HERE'S WHAT YOU DO

Whisk together the peanut butter and water in a small bowl until smooth. Add the soy sauce, honey, and lime juice, and whisk again.

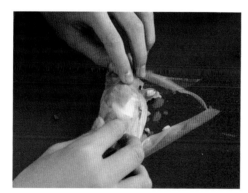

5

Fold the sides in and roll the wrapper up around the filling as shown. Set it aside and repeat soaking and filling the wrappers until you've used up all the wrappers and filling. Cut the spring rolls in half. Serve with the dipping sauce.

IRIS'S CORN & BLACK BEAN SALAD

Makes 6 to 8 servings

This recipe, from 12-year-old Iris, has loads of corn, tomatoes, and other veggies that come from her family's farm share (that's a weekly box of seasonal vegetables from a local farm). Iris likes to serve this salad with tortilla chips on the side. She also recommends putting it in burritos or topping nachos with it.

Here's What You Need

- 2 avocados, pitted, peeled, and diced (see page 89)
- Juice of 1 lime
- 1 (15.5-ounce) can black beans
- 2 cups frozen or fresh corn (thawed if frozen)
- 1 tomato, diced
- 1 red or green bell pepper, diced
- 3 garlic cloves, crushed
- 2 tablespoons chopped fresh cilantro
- 1 teaspoon cumin
- 1 teaspoon salt
- ¼ teaspoon black pepper

HERE'S WHAT YOU DO

1 Put the diced avocados in a large bowl and pour the lime juice over them. Toss gently to coat.

2 Open the can of black beans. Rinse and drain the beans in a colander in the sink. Add them to the bowl with the avocados.

3 Add the corn, tomato, bell pepper, garlic, cilantro, cumin, salt, and black pepper.

4 Stir well. Chill until ready to eat!

HOW TO . . .

PREPARE FRESH CORN

Fresh corn tastes best in Iris's salad. Pull off the green husk, pick off the silk, and break off the stalk end. It's a good idea to shuck it outside where you don't have to worry too much about cleaning up all those silky threads.

Cook the cobs in boiling water for just a couple of minutes.

When the cobs are cool, carefully cut the kernels off with a knife on a cutting board. Or try this trick: Put the cob in the tube of a Bundt pan to hold it steady while you cut!

FRIED RICE 🥄🥄🥄

Makes 4 servings

If you have leftover rice from last night's dinner, turn it into tonight's side dish with this Chinese restaurant favorite. Make sure to use cold rice instead of warm rice so that the finished dish is not mushy.

Here's What You Need

2	tablespoons vegetable oil
½	teaspoon sesame oil
4	scallions, sliced
1	cup frozen peas
1	medium carrot, peeled and grated
1	tablespoon grated fresh ginger
1	garlic clove, crushed
3	cups cooked and chilled white rice
3	large eggs
1½–2	tablespoons soy sauce

HERE'S WHAT YOU DO

1 Heat 1½ tablespoons of the vegetable oil and all of the sesame oil in a large wok or skillet over medium heat.

2 Slowly and carefully (to avoid being splattered by hot oil!) add the scallions, peas, carrot, ginger, and garlic. Sauté the vegetables for a minute, stirring constantly.

3

Add the rice and heat for 2 to 3 minutes, stirring occasionally.

4

Break the eggs into a small bowl. Beat them with a fork or small whisk.

5

Push the rice to the edges of the pan and pour the remaining ½ tablespoon vegetable oil into the center. Add the eggs and stir until they are cooked and scrambled.

6

Stir the eggs into the rice until everything is mixed up. Add the soy sauce and heat for another minute or two, stirring often. Serve and pass additional soy sauce.

COOK RICE

Cooked just right, plain rice makes a tasty, healthy side dish. It can also be the basis for all kinds of meals because it mixes well with so many different ingredients and sauces.

Here's how to cook it.

* Depending on which kind of rice you make, 1 cup uncooked rice will make 3 to 4 cups when cooked.

* Bring 2 cups water to a boil.

* Add 1 cup rice, stir, cover, and reduce the heat to low.

* Simmer for 15 to 20 minutes, until all the water is absorbed. (Brown rice takes 30 to 35 minutes to cook.)

Chicken Curry, page 138

CHAPTER SIX

MY FIRST DINNERS

What's for dinner? Your parents would probably be thrilled if you offered to cook your family dinner! Shoo them out of the kitchen and look for a recipe to make. On the following pages, you'll find recipes for favorite restaurant foods (see Sushi! California Rolls on page 136 and Fantastic Fish Tacos on page 140). You'll also find healthy versions of fast foods (see Super Sliders on page 134 and Popcorn Chicken on page 130). When your dinner's ready to serve, light the candles and call everyone down to a family dinner, compliments of the chef!

SPOON

* Bow-Tie Pasta with Tomatoes, Basil & Fresh Mozzarella
* Perfect Pesto!

 **SPOONS**

* Meatballs with Creamy Sauce
* Cheesy Bean Quesadillas
* Nutty Noodles
* Popcorn Chicken
* Mix-and-Match Pizza Party

 SPOONS

* Super Sliders
* Sushi! California Rolls
* Chicken Curry
* Fantastic Fish Tacos
* Excellent Egg Rolls
* Pizza Soup
* Cheesy Broccoli Soup

BOW-TIE PASTA
WITH TOMATOES, BASIL & FRESH MOZZARELLA

Makes 4 servings

Here's an easy, no-cook pasta sauce. (But don't forget to cook the pasta!) This recipe calls for bow-tie pasta, but you can use any fun shape that you like. You can also eat it without the noodles as an appetizer (in Italian, this salad is called insalata caprese). Or try it on some toasted Italian bread.

HERE'S WHAT YOU DO

1 Cut the mozzarella into bite-size pieces and place in a large serving bowl.

2 Snip the basil leaves with clean scissors and measure about ⅓ cup into the bowl.

3 Add the oil, tomatoes, garlic, and salt to the bowl. Stir well and add more salt to taste. Set aside to let the flavors blend together while you cook the pasta.

4 Have an adult help you cook the pasta (see How to Cook Pasta, page 123). Drain, then toss the warm noodles with the mozzarella and tomato mixture.

5 Serve on plates, and garnish with any remaining basil, if you like. Pass the parmesan, please!

Here's What You Need

½ pound fresh mozzarella
  Small bunch of fresh basil
¼ cup olive oil
2 large ripe tomatoes, chopped
1 garlic clove, crushed
1 teaspoon salt
1 (1-pound) box bow-tie pasta
  Grated parmesan cheese, for serving

PERFECT PESTO!

Makes 1 cup

Summer is the perfect time to make Perfect Pesto! Serve it up fresh on pasta. It tastes great on homemade pizza, too. Make extra to store in the freezer to enjoy in the winter months.

Here's What You Need

- 2 cups fresh basil leaves
- ¼ cup pine nuts, walnuts, or sunflower seeds
- 1 garlic clove, crushed
- ¾ cup olive oil
- ½ cup grated parmesan cheese
- 1 teaspoon salt
- Cooked pasta, for serving

HERE'S WHAT YOU DO

1 Put the basil leaves, pine nuts or other nuts or seeds, and crushed garlic into a food processor. Process until the leaves are all chopped up.

2 Pour the oil into the top of the food processor with the motor running. Turn off the motor and scrape the sides, then add the parmesan and salt. Process until smooth.

3 Toss it with cooked pasta (see How to Cook Pasta, page 123), and serve.

Rohan's Perfect PESTO

PASTA SHAPES

Pasta comes in all shapes and sizes. Take a look at the classic pasta shapes on this page, then check to see what you have in your own kitchen cupboard. When you cook, be sure to check the cooking times listed on the box. The time will vary depending on the thickness and variety of the pasta.

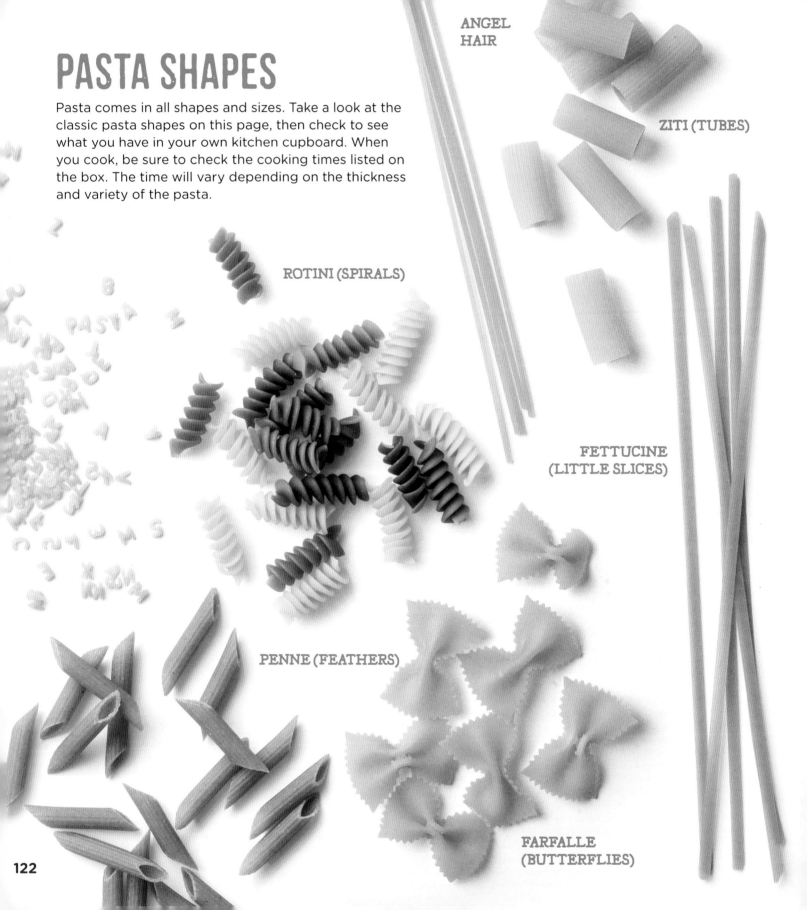

ANGEL HAIR

ZITI (TUBES)

ROTINI (SPIRALS)

FETTUCINE (LITTLE SLICES)

PENNE (FEATHERS)

FARFALLE (BUTTERFLIES)

HOW TO...
COOK PASTA

1 Fill a large pot with water. Bring it to a boil over high heat. The large pot is important so that the pasta has plenty of room to cook and doesn't stick together. When the water begins to boil, add 1 teaspoon salt.

2 Carefully add the pasta and bring the water back to a boil. Lower the heat to medium-high. Stir frequently during the first few minutes and occasionally at the end.

3 Set the timer. Look on the box for the recommended cooking time for the type of pasta you are cooking; linguine, shells, and fettuccine, for example, have very different cooking times.

4 When the timer goes off, give it a taste test. If you like the texture, drain the pasta (or ask an adult to do it for you). To do this, set a colander in the sink and carefully carry the pot over to the sink. Be sure no one is standing in the way! Practice doing this with adult supervision a few times, as carrying hot water can be dangerous. Toss the drained pasta immediately in your sauce and serve.

CREATIVE COOKS!

THE SECRET IS IN THE SAUCE

Serve your freshly cooked pasta with any of these sauces.

* Pesto (see page 121)

* Tomatoes, basil, and mozzarella (see page 120)

* Marinara and meatballs

* Butter and parmesan cheese

* Olive oil, sautéed garlic, and salt

* Alfredo sauce and bacon

* Peanut sauce (see page 113)

TIP: Reserve 1 cup of pasta water from the pot. That way, if your pasta gets too sticky or your sauce needs thinning, you can add a splash of pasta water without diluting the flavor.

MEATBALLS
WITH CREAMY SAUCE

Makes about 40 meatballs

These mini meatballs with tasty cream sauce make a full meal. If you don't want to make the sauce, you can serve the meatballs with pasta sauce instead. Or serve them as a finger food on a stick (see opposite page).

Here's What You Need

MEATBALLS
- ½ cup breadcrumbs
- ¼ cup milk
- 1 pound ground beef
- 1 pound ground pork
- 1 egg, beaten
- 1 teaspoon salt
- ¼ teaspoon black pepper

CREAMY SAUCE
- 1 cup beef stock
- 1 cup heavy cream
- 3 tablespoons flour
- 1 tablespoon soy sauce

  Cooked noodles, for serving, optional

Preheat the oven to 400°F (200°C).

HERE'S WHAT YOU DO

1 Mix the breadcrumbs and milk in a small bowl and let soak for a few minutes.

2 Place the ground beef and pork in a large bowl. Add the egg, salt, pepper, and breadcrumb mixture. Mix with a large spoon (or clean hands).

3 Shape the mixture into 1-inch meatballs, and place the balls on an ungreased baking sheet.

4 Bake for 15 minutes, or until the meatballs are cooked through and no longer pink in the middle.

5 Meanwhile, whisk the beef stock, cream, flour, and soy sauce in a large saucepan. Cook over low heat, stirring, until the sauce is creamy and thick, about 10 minutes.

6 Add the meatballs to the pan, and coat them in the sauce. Cook until the meatballs are hot. Serve over noodles, if you like.

MEATBALLS ON A STICK!

For fun, serve your meatballs on a stick! Thread cooked meatballs and sliced bell peppers on a skewer. Or you could try cooked pasta, mozzarella balls, and fresh basil. Serve the sticks with warmed pasta sauce on the side for dipping.

CHEESY BEAN QUESADILLAS

Makes 4 quesadillas

For a quick school-night supper, cook a batch of these cheesy quesadillas. Serve them with Gorgeous Garden Salsa (page 90) and Mean Green Guacamole (page 88).

Here's What You Need

8 flour tortillas
1 (15.5-ounce) can refried beans
1½ cups shredded Monterey Jack cheese
1½ teaspoons butter

HERE'S WHAT YOU DO

1 Place a tortilla on a plate or cutting board. Add a few spoonfuls of refried beans and spread them out with the back of the spoon. Sprinkle evenly with some of the shredded cheese. Place a second tortilla on top.

2 Melt the butter on a griddle or in a skillet over medium heat. Place a quesadilla in the skillet. Cook until the cheese begins to melt and the bottom tortilla is light brown.

3 Flip and cook on the other side until light brown. Repeat with the rest of the ingredients to make three more quesadillas.

4 Remove the quesadilla from the pan and place on a cutting board. Use a pizza cutter to cut it into wedges.

5 Arange the wedges on a plate and serve with salsa and/or guacamole.

CRAZY QUESADILLAS

FLOWER FUN

Arrange the quesadilla wedges like petals around a tiny bowl of salsa. Add a cilantro leaf stem.

FLUTTER AWAY

To make a butterfly, cut the quesadilla in half. Add an olive head, cilantro stem antennae, and some corn and tomato spots.

Hold one stick in the crook of the thumb with it resting on the third finger.

Hold the other stick between the tip of the thumb and the first two fingers.

Practice bringing the two sticks together while picking up Nutty Noodles, just like Ernnie!

NUTTY NOODLES

Makes 4 to 6 servings

Make these restaurant-style noodles at home with this easy recipe. You can buy Chinese noodles in the refrigerator section of most grocery stores.

Here's What You Need

1 pound Chinese noodles
¼ cup creamy peanut butter
½ cup warm water
¼ cup soy sauce
1 tablespoon peeled and chopped fresh ginger
1 garlic clove, crushed

HERE'S WHAT YOU DO

1

Cook the noodles according to the package directions. Drain and rinse with cold water.

2

In a large bowl, use a fork or whisk to stir the peanut butter with the water until it is creamy.

PEANUT NOODLE TOPPINGS

* Grated carrot

* Scallions (sliced into rounds)

* Cucumber (peeled, seeded, and thinly sliced)

* Chopped roasted peanuts

* Toasted sesame seeds

* Steamed edamame

* Steamed broccoli florets

* Fresh-squeezed lime juice

* Thinly sliced green or red bell peppers

3 Stir in the soy sauce, ginger, and garlic.

4 Add the noodles to the bowl. Toss well and serve with toppings on the side (see Creative Cooks!).

POPCORN CHICKEN

Makes 4 servings

Don't chicken out! It's easy to make your own fried chicken bites for dinner. Instead of the usual old chicken fingers, though, make your meal extra fun by cutting the chicken into bite-size chunks to make Popcorn Chicken to dunk into different sauces.

Here's What You Need

- 1 pound boneless, skinless chicken breasts, cut into 1-inch pieces
- 1 egg
- 2 tablespoons milk
- ½ teaspoon salt
- Pinch of black pepper
- 1½ cups seasoned breadcrumbs
- 2 tablespoons olive oil

HERE'S WHAT YOU DO

1 Put the chicken pieces in a bowl. Mix the egg, milk, salt, and pepper in another bowl. Pour the breadcrumbs into a third bowl.

2 Line up the three bowls. Dip each piece of chicken first into the egg wash, then into the breadcrumbs.

3 When all the pieces are coated, heat the oil in a large skillet over medium-high heat.

4

Add the chicken and cook until golden, about 3 minutes on each side.

5

Transfer the cooked chicken to a serving plate. Set it out with a variety of dipping sauces and dive in!

TAKE A DIP!

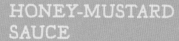

Serve your chicken fingers with one of these tasty dips.

HONEY-MUSTARD SAUCE

Mix together ⅓ cup mustard with 1 to 2 tablespoons honey.

BUFFALO SAUCE

Whisk 3 tablespoons melted butter with 1 teaspoon cayenne pepper. Mix in 2 teaspoons white vinegar and a pinch of salt.

CURRY MAYO

Mix ½ cup mayonnaise with 1 tablespoon curry powder and 1 to 2 teaspoons milk until creamy.

TIP: You can also use these dips with veggies!

131

MIX-AND-MATCH
PIZZA PARTY

Keep your party simple by starting with store-bought pizza dough. Bring the dough to room temperature, then flatten it on an oiled baking sheet. Spread with tomato sauce and add your favorite toppings. Bake for 15 to 20 minutes in an oven preheated to 400°F (200°C). Slice it up and enjoy!

HERE KITTY-KITTY PIZZA

Pizza Dough + Tomato Sauce + Pepperoni Whiskers + Olive Eyes & Nose

PLAIN AND SIMPLE PIZZA

Pizza Dough + Tomato Sauce + Shredded Mozzarella

PIZZA SELF-PORTRAITS
Pizza Dough + Tomato Sauce + Assorted Veggies

MARGHERITA PIZZA

Pizza Dough + Fresh Basil + Tomato Sauce + Fresh Mozzarella

DINNER TABLE FUN

Make the dinner table talk fun with a conversation jar. Cut out the cards in the back of the book. Make up a few more of your own if you like. Place them in a jar and add a label that says "Table Talk!" Now take turns reaching in and answering the questions, like "If you had a kitchen superpower, what would it be?"

IF YOU WERE A FOOD, what would you be?

Which flavor do you like better, **CHOCOLATE** or **VANILLA**?

Are you a **LEFTY** or a **RIGHTY**? Try eating your dinner with your fork or spoon in the other hand!

SUPER SLIDERS III

Makes 4 servings

Mix up a batch of mini burgers—also known as sliders—with a few easy ingredients. Have an older sibling or a grown-up help you grill the burgers outside. Serve them on dinner rolls, add toppings, and pass the ketchup!

Here's What You Need

- 1½ pounds ground beef
- 1 egg
- ⅓ cup breadcrumbs
- 1 garlic clove, crushed
- 2 teaspoons dried oregano
- ½ teaspoon salt
- 8 small slices cheese (your favorite), optional
- 8 dinner rolls

SLIDER TOPPINGS

Pickles	Bacon
Ketchup	Chopped onion
Lettuce	Relish
Tomato slices	

HERE'S WHAT YOU DO

1 Put the ground beef, egg, bread-crumbs, garlic, oregano, and salt in a large bowl.

2 Mix everything together with your (clean!) hands or a wooden spoon.

3 Shape the meat mixture into 8 patties. Wash your hands again!

4 Heat the grill to medium-high. When it's nice and hot, grill the burgers for about 3 minutes on each side. (Tip: Use a long-handled grill spatula for flipping the sliders.)

5 To make cheeseburgers, if you like, top with mini slices of cheese after you flip the burgers. Let the cheese melt for a minute or two while the burgers finish cooking.

6 Cut the dinner rolls in half and place a burger on each one. Put the burgers on a serving platter.

7 Serve the burgers and let everyone pile on the toppings.

SLIDER CAFÉ!

Looking for a little neighborhood fun? Open up a slider restaurant at home!

* Set up a table with colorful paper plates and napkins.

* Grab a pad of paper for taking orders.

* Ask your customers what toppings they'd like on their burgers or cheeseburgers. Write it down on your order pad.

* Cook the sliders, add the toppings, then serve them up with a fun flag (find them in the back of the book).

* When your customers have finished eating, clear the table. They might leave you a tip!

SUSHI! CALIFORNIA ROLLS

Makes 8 rolls

You don't have to go out when you're craving sushi for dinner. Stock up on nori seaweed, sushi rice, and a bamboo mat in the Asian section of your grocery store and try making it at home. Are you ready to roll?

Here's What You Need

- 1 cucumber
- 4 sticks imitation crabmeat (also called surimi)
- 1 avocado
- 3 tablespoons rice vinegar
- 1½ teaspoons sugar
- ¼ teaspoon salt
- 4 cups cooked sushi rice, made a day in advance (2 cups uncooked)
- 4 sheets nori
- Toasted sesame seeds
- Soy sauce, wasabi, and pickled ginger, for serving

SPECIAL EQUIPMENT
Bamboo sushi mat

HERE'S WHAT YOU DO

1 Cut the cucumber lengthwise into spears. Cut the crab sticks into small strips. Slice the avocado into ¼-inch-thick pieces (see page 89). Set the ingredients on a large platter.

2 Mix the vinegar, sugar, and salt in a small bowl. Pour it over the cooled sushi rice and stir to combine.

3 Cover both sides of a bamboo sushi mat with plastic wrap. Cut the nori sheets in half lengthwise and lay one piece on the mat, shiny side down.

4 Dip your hands into a bowl of warm water to prevent the rice from sticking to them, and pick up a handful of the rice about the size of baseball. Evenly spread the rice onto the nori, leaving a small uncovered area around the edges.

5 Sprinkle the rice with some sesame seeds. Flip the nori over carefully so that the rice side faces the mat.

6 Place a few pieces each of the crab sticks, avocado, and cucumber onto the nori, about 1 inch from the edge closest to you.

6 Roll up the sushi by slowly folding the mat over the filling, pushing gently to form it into a log. Don't roll the sushi mat under as you press. Lift the mat and move it forward as you roll up the sushi.

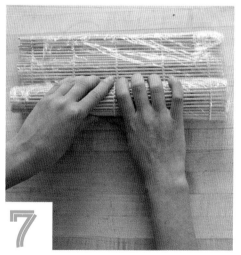

7 Continue rolling and pressing slightly until you form a log. Repeat with the remaining ingredients to make 8 rolls.

8 Cut each roll into 6 pieces. For easy slicing, dip the knife in hot water first. Serve the sushi on plates with soy sauce, wasabi, and pickled ginger on the side.

CHICKEN CURRY

Makes 4 servings

Curry powder is the secret to this flavorful chicken dish. Many spices are in curry powder—cardamom, turmeric, cumin, coriander, cloves, and more. You can buy lots of different kinds of premade curry powder at the grocery store.

Here's What You Need

- 1 tablespoon vegetable oil
- 1 small onion, chopped
- 1 garlic clove, crushed
- 1 tablespoon curry powder
- ½ teaspoon salt
- 1 whole boneless, skinless chicken breast, cut into 2-inch chunks
- 1 cup coconut milk
  Hot cooked rice

1 Heat the oil in a large skillet over medium-high heat. Add the onion and garlic, and sauté for 5 minutes.

2 Stir in the curry powder and salt.

3 Add the chicken and sauté until the outside is golden brown, about 5 minutes.

4 Pour the coconut milk over the chicken.

5 Bring the coconut milk to a boil, then reduce the heat to low.

6 Simmer, uncovered, stirring occasionally, until the chicken is cooked through, about 10 minutes. Serve hot over cooked rice.

FANTASTIC FISH TACOS

Makes 8 to 10 tacos

This Tex-Mex favorite starts with a rub—a simple spice mix that you spread on the fish before you cook it. You can also spread the rub on steak or chicken. Once it's cooked, wrap up the fish in warm corn tortillas and add your favorite toppings.

Here's What You Need

- 1 tablespoon chili powder
- 1 tablespoon cumin
- ½ teaspoon salt
- 1 pound haddock or other firm white fish
- 2 tablespoons vegetable oil
- 8–10 corn tortillas
- Toppings (see Creative Cooks!)

Preheat the oven to 300°F (150°C).

HERE'S WHAT YOU DO

1 Mix the chili powder, cumin, and salt on a large plate. Cover both sides of the fish with the spice mixture.

2 Heat the oil in a large skillet over medium-high heat. Add the fish and cook on both sides until white in the center. The time will vary depending on the thickness of the fish, but it should be 2 to 3 minutes per side.

3 Remove the fish from the skillet and place on a serving plate. Let it cool slightly, then gently pull it apart into shreds or chunks with a fork.

4 Wrap the tortillas in aluminum foil and warm them in the oven for about 10 minutes.

5 Set out a variety of toppings in bowls and let everyone create their own combinations.

TACO TOPPING BAR

These toppings make delicious additions to your fish tacos. Choose any combo you like—Sophie likes extra cheese!

* Shredded cabbage

* Grated Monterey Jack cheese

* Iris's Corn & Black Bean Salad (page 114)

* Gorgeous Garden Salsa (page 90)

* Mean Green Guacamole (page 88)

* Chili-lime cream: In a small bowl, stir together ½ cup sour cream, 2 teaspoons fresh-squeezed lime juice, ½ crushed garlic clove, ½ teaspoon chili powder, and salt to taste.

EXCELLENT EGG ROLLS

Makes 12 egg rolls

Do you like to order egg rolls at Chinese restaurants? If so, try making them at home. You can find egg roll wrappers in the refrigerated section of most grocery stores.

Here's What You Need

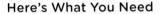

- 1 tablespoon vegetable oil, plus ¼ cup for frying
- 2 teaspoons sesame oil
- 2 garlic cloves, finely chopped
- 1 tablespoon peeled and chopped fresh ginger
- 1 (1-pound) container firm tofu, cubed
- 4 cups thinly sliced green cabbage (about 1 small head)
- 1 cup grated carrots (about 3 carrots)
- 2 tablespoons soy sauce, plus more for dipping
- 1 (1-pound) package square egg roll wrappers

HERE'S WHAT YOU DO

1 Heat the 1 tablespoon vegetable oil and the sesame oil in a large skillet over medium-high heat. Add the garlic and ginger, and cook for about 1 minute.

2 Add the tofu, cabbage, and carrots. Cook, stirring often, until the veggies are soft, about 10 minutes. Then stir in the soy sauce. Turn off the heat and let cool.

3 Lay an egg roll wrapper diagonally on a cutting board. Spread the filling in a corner of the wrapper, leaving room on the edges. Set a little bowl of water near your work space.

4 Fold the corner nearest you over the filling.

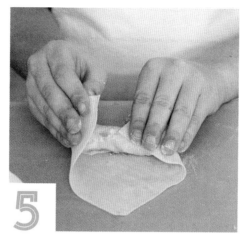

5 Fold the two sides over the center, sealing them by rubbing with a wet fingertip.

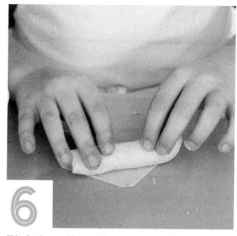

6 Tightly roll up the egg roll. Seal the edge. Repeat with the remaining wrappers.

7 Heat the ¼ cup vegetable oil in a large skillet over medium heat. Using tongs, carefully lower 4 or 5 egg rolls one at a time into the hot oil. Fry until golden brown on one side, about 3 minutes. Turn and fry for about 3 minutes longer. If the egg rolls are browning too quickly, lower the heat to medium-low.

8 As each egg roll finishes frying, remove it to drain on paper towels. Add uncooked rolls, without crowding the pan, until they are all cooked.

9 Transfer the egg rolls to a plate and serve with extra soy sauce for dipping.

PIZZA SOUP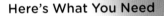

Serves 4 to 6

Cook up a twist on pasta e fagioli, a classic Italian dish of pasta and beans!

Here's What You Need

- 1 pound ground beef or ground Italian sausage
- 2 garlic cloves, crushed
- ⅔ cup diced onion (about 1 small onion)
- 2 cups beef broth
- 1 (28-ounce) can crushed tomatoes
- 1 (8-ounce) can tomato sauce
- 1 (15.5-ounce) can kidney or cannellini beans, drained
- 1 tablespoon each dried basil and oregano
  Salt and black pepper
- 1 cup dried mini pasta shells

HERE'S WHAT YOU DO

1 Brown the ground beef or sausage in a soup pot over medium heat. Cook, stirring occasionally, until no longer pink, about 5 minutes.

2 Add the crushed garlic and diced onion, and cook for another 5 minutes. Stir often.

3

Add the broth, crushed tomatoes, tomato sauce, beans, and dried basil and oregano. Add salt and pepper to taste.

4

Stir to combine all the ingredients. Turn the heat to low and simmer for 20 minutes.

5

While the soup is simmering, cook the pasta. Fill a pot halfway with water and bring it to a boil. Add the pasta and cook for 8 to 10 minutes. Drain the pasta in a colander set in the sink.

6

Serve the soup in bowls. Add some pasta shells to each bowl. Garnish with mozzarella and other toppings, if you like.

GET CREATIVE!

Before eating your pizza soup, garnish the bowl with any of the following toppings:

SHREDDED MOZZARELLA CHEESE

SNIPPED FRESH PARSLEY OR BASIL

PESTO

CROUTONS

145

CHEESY BROCCOLI SOUP

Makes 4 to 6 servings

This soup is so creamy and tasty, you won't even know you're eating broccoli and carrots for dinner! As you make it, you'll practice lots of cooking skills including chopping onions, crushing garlic, and grating carrots, plus using a blender. Soup's on!

Here's What You Need

- 4 tablespoons butter
- ½ cup chopped onion
- 1 garlic clove, crushed
- ¼ cup flour
- 2 cups milk
- ½ cup half-and-half
- 4 cups vegetable or chicken broth
- 4 cups broccoli florets
- 1 cup grated carrots
- 8 ounces grated cheddar cheese
- Salt and black pepper

A ROUX (pronounced RUE) is a heated mixture of butter and flour used to thicken soups, sauces, and gravies.

HERE'S WHAT YOU DO

1 Melt the butter in a soup pot over medium heat. Add the onion and garlic, and cook for about 5 minutes, or until tender.

2 Sprinkle in the flour, and whisk for a few minutes to create a roux.

3 Slowly stir in the milk and half-and-half. Add the broth and bring the mixture to a boil over medium-high heat. Lower the heat and simmer for 15 minutes.

4 Add the broccoli and carrots. Simmer the soup for 20 to 25 minutes, or until the broccoli is soft.

5 Pour the soup into a blender and purée to the thickness you like (work in batches). Put the soup back in the pot.

6 Stir in the cheese. Simmer for 10 minutes. Just before serving, taste the soup. Add salt and pepper to taste. You can add extra milk to thin the soup, if you like.

MAKE A BREAD BOWL

It's easy to create your own restaurant-style serving bowl. Start with a small round loaf of bread for each serving and follow the tips below.

* Cut a ½–inch-thick slice from the top of the loaf with a serrated knife.

* Scoop out the middle of the loaf with your (clean!) hands, leaving about ¾ inch of bread for the sides of bowl.

* Fill the bread bowl with hot soup and serve right away. Nibble on the bread top as you enjoy your soup!

148　　　　Meringue Nests, page 168

CHAPTER SEVEN

TIME FOR DESSERT

What's the sweetest part about learning to cook? Making desserts, of course! In this chapter, you'll find out how to mix up homemade chocolate candy, bake lemon squares, whip up a batch of carrot cupcakes, and make other delicious treats. In no time, your kitchen will become a bakery filled with sweet smells and yummy tastes. Stand back and watch the crowds swarm in!

SPOON

* Dipped Strawberry Dessert

* Mix-and-Match Chocolate Factory

* Cream Cheese Frosting

SPOONS

* Hot Cocoa Pops

* Very Vanilla Pudding

* Snickerdoodles

* Chocolate Chip Cookie Factory

* Amazing Apple Crisp

* One-Bowl Chocolate Cupcakes

SPOONS

* Little Lemon Squares

* Meringue Nests

* Maisie's Carrot Cupcakes

DIPPED STRAWBERRY DESSERT

Makes 6 servings

This is a fun, elegant dessert to serve when fresh strawberries are in season. Pick up a few pints of berries from a farmers' market or pick-your-own farm. All you do is dip the berries into cream and shaved chocolate to make a delicious treat.

Here's What You Need

- ¼ cup heavy cream
- ¼ cup sour cream
- 1 (3.5-ounce) high-quality dark chocolate bar
- ½ cup confectioners' sugar
- 2 pints strawberries (dry them after washing and leave the stems on)

HERE'S WHAT YOU DO

1 Whisk the heavy cream and sour cream together in a small bowl until smooth. Cover and refrigerate for a few hours.

2 Working over waxed paper, grate the chocolate bar with a cheese grater or vegetable peeler. Pour the shavings into a small bowl.

3 Sift the confectioners' sugar onto a separate sheet of waxed paper. Transfer it to a small bowl.

4 Arrange the bowls of cream, grated chocolate, and confectioners' sugar in the middle of a platter, with the strawberries around them. Let the dipping party begin! Dip the strawberries into the cream, then into the sugar, and finally into the chocolate.

HOST A TEA PARTY!

Having a fancy tea party, like Abby and Maddie did, is a fun way to do something different with your friends. Here are some tips for creating an elegant afternoon.

* Send out invitations with the time and place, if you like.

* Dress up the table with a tablecloth and vase of flowers.

* Set the table with real teacups and saucers.

* Make Tea Party Sandwiches (page 57) and serve Dipped Strawberry Dessert.

* Serve herbal tea or juice in teacups.

* Practice a little tea party etiquette (napkins in lap, hold teacups by the handles, take small bites, and don't forget to say "Please pass the tea!").

* Pick a theme: Try a garden tea party, a vintage tea, a fairy tea, or even a teddy bear tea for your little sister!

HOW TO...
MELT CHOCOLATE

1 Place 1 cup chocolate chips in a microwave-safe bowl (not metal!). Microwave on high power for 1 minute. Stir the partially melted chips, then microwave for another 30 seconds and stir again.

2 Are the chocolate chips melted? If so, you can use them in your chocolate factory. If not, return the bowl to the microwave and zap the chips for another 15 seconds.

NOTE: Chocolate chips can burn pretty easily, so once they start to melt, zap them for only a few seconds at a time, and keep checking and stirring.

MIX-AND-MATCH
CHOCOLATE FACTORY

Making homemade candy is a snap. Follow the directions in How to Melt Chocolate at left, then open up your candy factory. Begin with some of these sweet treats. You can get creative and invent your own chocolates. Have any white chocolate chips? Try some white chocolate candies, too!

COOKIE CRUNCH
Graham Crackers + Chocolate + Crushed Mint Candies

GREAT GRAHAMS
Graham Crackers + White Chocolate + Mini M&M's

MONKEY BITES
Frozen Bananas + Chocolate

PARTY PRETZELS

Thin Pretzels + Chocolate +
Rainbow Sprinkles

CONE SPECIAL

Ice Cream Cone
+ Chocolate + Sprinkles

APRICOT DELIGHT

Dried Apricots
+ White Chocolate

MARSHMALLOW MADNESS

Marshmallows + Chocolate +
Rainbow Sprinkles

SWEET SPUDS

Potato Chips
+ Chocolate

HOT COCOA POPS

Makes 2 cups hot cocoa or 4 frozen cocoa pops

Cook up some hot cocoa—and pour yourself a cup. Then freeze the rest for ice pops. That way, you'll get to enjoy both hot and cold cocoa!

Here's What You Need

- 2 tablespoons unsweetened cocoa powder
- ¼ cup confectioners' sugar
- 2 cups milk
- ½ teaspoon vanilla extract
- 1 cup mini marshmallows

SPECIAL EQUIPMENT
Ice-pop molds

HERE'S WHAT YOU DO

1 Whisk the cocoa powder and confectioners' sugar together in a medium saucepan.

2 Slowly pour in the milk, whisking the whole time to mix the dry ingredients completely into the liquid. Stir in the vanilla.

3 Cook the cocoa over medium heat until it just starts to boil, then turn off the heat. You can serve yourself a cup right now, if you want!

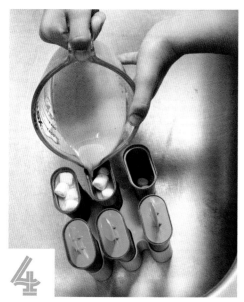

4 Let the cocoa cool. Put a few mini marshmallows into each ice-pop mold, then fill them with cocoa. Do this step in the sink, in case you spill! Add the tops and insert the sticks.

5 Freeze overnight. Remove the pops from the molds by running them under warm water. Enjoy on a hot day!

HOT COCOA MIX

Looking for a holiday gift for your teacher? Make your own hot cocoa mix. Combine the cocoa powder and confectioners' sugar from the Here's What You Need list in a bowl. Package it in a plastic bag tied with ribbon and tuck the bag into a special mug.

Write out these directions on a recipe card: "Add 2 cups milk and ½ teaspoon vanilla extract." Now the mug and mix are ready to give to your teacher.

TIP: If you want to give more hot cocoa mix, double or triple the recipe and put it in a glass container tied with a bow.

VERY VANILLA PUDDING

Makes 4 servings

Just when you think there's nothing in the house for dessert, think again. If you have milk, eggs, and sugar, you can stir up your very own homemade pudding!

Here's What You Need

⅔ cup sugar
¼ cup cornstarch
⅛ teaspoon salt
3 cups milk
3 egg yolks
2 teaspoons vanilla extract
Toppings (see below)

PUDDING TOPPINGS

* Banana slices
* Maple sugar
* Blueberries
* Sliced strawberries
* Raspberries
* Whipped cream
* Mini chocolate chips
* Cookie crumbs
* Chocolate sprinkles

HERE'S WHAT YOU DO

1 In a medium saucepan, whisk together the sugar, cornstarch, and salt. Add the milk and egg yolks, and whisk until thoroughly combined.

2 Heat the pudding over medium heat, stirring until it thickens and bubbles, 5 to 7 minutes. Continue cooking for 1 minute longer, stirring to keep the pudding from coming to a full boil.

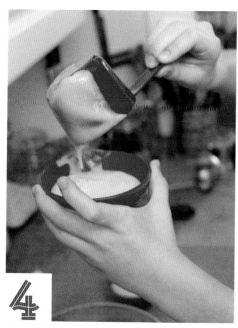

3

Turn off the heat. Stir in the vanilla.

4

Pour the pudding into small bowls while it's still warm. Refrigerate until set, at least 1 hour. (You can also eat it warm!) Decorate your portion with any combination of toppings.

HOW TO...

SEPARATE EGGS

Sometimes you need to use only part of an egg in a recipe. For example, the yolks add creaminess and a nice color to puddings, and the whites give meringues (see page 168) the fluffiness they need to hold their shape. Separating eggs may seem tricky, but it's pretty easy once you've practiced a few times.

1

Have two small, clean, dry bowls ready. Crack an egg on the side of one bowl. Your goal is to crack the shell evenly into two halves without crushing it.

2

As you separate the shell pieces, hold one upright to contain the yolk, letting the egg white spill into a bowl.

3

Gently slide the egg yolk between the two shells, letting more of the egg white fall into the bowl. Be careful not to let a sharp point of the shell break the yolk.

4

Drop the yolk into a separate bowl. If any of the yolk falls into the egg white, the whites won't whip up properly, so be very careful.

SNICKERDOODLES

Makes 2 to 3 dozen cookies

These buttery cookies are fun to make—you get to roll them in cinnamon sugar before baking! And they travel well. Treat your teammates to them after a good game!

Here's What You Need

COOKIE DOUGH
- 1⅓ cups flour
- ¾ teaspoon baking powder
- ⅛ teaspoon salt
- ½ cup (1 stick) butter, softened
- ¾ cup sugar
- 1 egg

TOPPING
- ¼ cup sugar
- 2 teaspoons cinnamon

Preheat the oven to 375°F (190°C).

HERE'S WHAT YOU DO

1 Stir the flour, baking powder, and salt in a medium bowl.

2 In a larger bowl, cream the butter and sugar with an electric mixer. Beat in the egg.

3 Gradually add the flour mixture, mixing well between additions.

4 Roll the dough into balls about 1½ inches wide.

5 To make the topping, mix the sugar and cinnamon in a shallow bowl. Roll the balls in the mixture.

6 Place them on an ungreased baking sheet, about 2 inches apart. (Line the baking sheet with parchment paper for easier cleanup.)

7 Gently flatten the cookies with the bottom of a glass. Bake for 7 to 10 minutes, or until brown on the edges. Let the cookies sit for 5 minutes on the pan, and then transfer them to a rack to cool completely.

CHOCOLATE CHIP COOKIE FACTORY 🍴

Makes 2 dozen cookies

Learn how to make this classic cookie so you can pack it in your lunch box all week long. Be sure to bring extras to share with friends at the lunch table!

Here's What You Need

2¼ cups flour	¾ cup packed brown sugar
1 teaspoon baking soda	2 eggs
⅔ teaspoon salt	1 teaspoon vanilla extract
1 cup (2 sticks) butter, softened	2 cups (16 ounces) chocolate chips
¾ cup granulated sugar	

Preheat the oven to 375°F (190°C).

CREATIVE COOKS!

COOKIE CREATIVITY

* Mix up the size and bake tiny or giant chocolate chip cookies. The baking time will be shorter for smaller cookies and longer for larger ones, so make sure all the cookies on each tray are the same size.

* Bake them on a stick! Slip a lollipop or ice-pop stick into the center before baking.

* Skip the chocolate chips and use white chocolate or butterscotch chips instead.

* Substitute peanut butter chips or toffee bits for half of the chocolate chips to make a candy bar version.

* Bake the dough in a greased 13- by 9- by 2-inch pan for 20 to 25 minutes to make chocolate chip cookie bars!

1 Stir the flour, baking soda, and salt in a medium bowl.

2 In a separate large mixing bowl, beat the butter and sugars with an electric mixer.

3 Beat in the eggs, one at a time. Stir in the vanilla.

4 Gradually beat in the flour mixture. Stir in the chocolate chips.

5 Drop the batter by rounded tablespoons onto ungreased baking sheets, using a cookie scoop or spoon. (Line the baking sheets with parchment paper for easier cleanup.)

6 Bake for 9 to 11 minutes, or until the cookies are just turning golden brown. Let them sit for 2 minutes, and then transfer them to a rack to cool completely.

APPLE CRISP INNOVATIONS

Try these variations on this classic recipe.

APPLE-CRANBERRY CRISP
Sprinkle ½ cup dried cranberries or dried cherries on top of the apples.

BLUEBERRY-PEACH CRISP
Instead of apples, use 3 sliced peaches and 2 cups blueberries.

APPLE CRISP PARFAIT
In a parfait glass, alternate layers of vanilla ice cream and apple crisp. Top with whipped cream and dig in!

AMAZING APPLE CRISP

Makes 6 to 8 servings

Pick your own apples and mix up this simple but satisfying dessert. The best part: the crumbled topping made with oats and cinnamon.

Here's What You Need

6 apples	3 tablespoons flour
1½ cups quick-cooking rolled oats	1 tablespoon cinnamon
¾ cup light brown sugar	½ cup (1 stick) butter, softened

Preheat the oven to 375°F (190°C).

HERE'S WHAT YOU DO

1 Peel the apples with an apple peeler.

2 Slice and core the apples with an apple slicer.

3 Spread them evenly in an 8- or 9-inch square baking pan.

4

Place the oats, brown sugar, flour, and cinnamon in a medium bowl and stir together.

5

Add the softened butter and cut with a pastry cutter until crumbly. Or mix it up with your (clean!) hands.

6

Crumble the topping evenly over the sliced apples. Bake for 40 to 45 minutes, until the topping is light brown and the juices start to bubble.

ONE-BOWL CHOCOLATE CUPCAKES

Makes 24 cupcakes

If you're in the mood for chocolate cupcakes, but you're out of milk, eggs, and butter, here's a quick and easy vegan recipe that will do the trick. Or you can use the same batter to make an equally quick and easy cake!

Here's What You Need

- 3 cups flour
- 2 cups sugar
- 2 teaspoons baking soda
- 1 teaspoon salt
- ¾ cup unsweetened cocoa powder
- 2 cups water
- ¾ cup vegetable or olive oil
- 2 tablespoons white vinegar
- 2 teaspoons vanilla extract

Preheat the oven to 350°F (180°C).

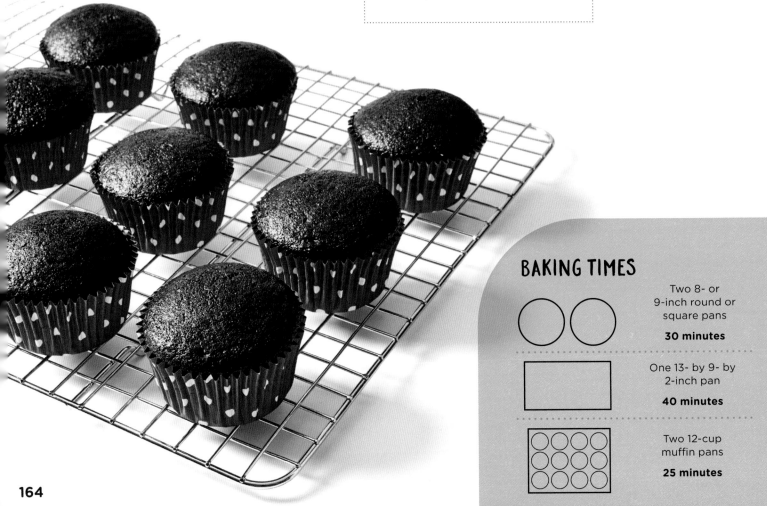

BAKING TIMES

Two 8- or 9-inch round or square pans

30 minutes

One 13- by 9- by 2-inch pan

40 minutes

Two 12-cup muffin pans

25 minutes

1 Line two 12-cup muffin pans with paper liners. If you're making a cake, grease the pan.

2 Stir the flour, sugar, baking soda, salt, and cocoa powder in a large bowl.

3 Add the water, oil, vinegar, and vanilla. Mix it up with a spoon until nice and smooth.

4 Pour the batter into the muffin cups until they are two-thirds full. Bake for 25 minutes (longer for a cake), or until a toothpick inserted in the center comes out clean.

I Love Chocolate

LITTLE LEMON SQUARES

Makes 24 bars

You've probably heard the saying "When life hands you lemons, make lemonade." Well, how about making lemon squares instead? These treats are sweet and sour at the same time. Sprinkle a little confectioners' sugar on top, and enjoy.

Here's What You Need

CRUST
- ¾ cup (1½ sticks) butter, softened
- 1½ cups flour
- ⅓ cup confectioners' sugar

FILLING
- 4 eggs
- 1¼ cups granulated sugar
- 1½ tablespoons lemon zest
- ⅓ cup fresh-squeezed lemon juice (from 2 or 3 lemons)
- ½ teaspoon vanilla extract
- ⅓ cup flour
- Confectioners' sugar, for dusting

Preheat the oven to 350°F (180°C).

HERE'S WHAT YOU DO

1 To make the crust, place the butter in a mixing bowl and blend with an electric mixer until fluffy, about 1 minute.

2 Add the flour and confectioners' sugar. Mix until it turns into a soft dough.

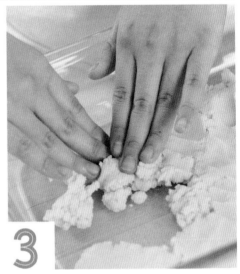

3 Press the dough into a 13- by 9-inch baking pan. Bake for 20 minutes, or until the edges start to brown. Take the pan out of the oven and let it cool.

4

While the crust is baking, mix the eggs and granulated sugar with a mixer. Add the lemon zest, lemon juice, and vanilla.

5

Mix in the flour.

6

Pour the filling over the cooled crust and tilt the pan to spread it evenly. Bake the bars until the filling is set, about 25 minutes.

7

Let the lemon squares cool slightly. Then dust them lightly with confectioners' sugar using a sifter. Slice into 24 small bars.

HOW TO...
MAKE LEMON ZEST

Lemon squares get their citrus flavor not just from lemon juice but from the peel, too. The zest is the yellow outer layer of the peel. Under that is the white pith, which is too bitter for cooking.

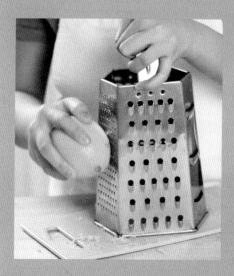

TO MAKE ZEST, wash the lemon and dry it off. Lightly rub the rind against the smallest holes of a grater as shown (or you can use a special zesting tool, rotating the lemon as you go to get every bit of the colored part).

After you zest a lemon, cut it in half and squeeze it for juice. You can zest fruit after you squeeze it, but it's easier the other way around.

MERINGUE NESTS

Makes 12 to 24 meringues, depending on their size

These French treats are light and sweet. Top them with fresh raspberries and mint for a fancy dessert to serve to your grandparents or other special guests when they come to visit.

Here's What You Need

2 egg whites
½ teaspoon cream of tartar
½ teaspoon vanilla extract
⅔ cup sugar

Whipped cream, for filling
1 pint fresh raspberries
1 bunch mint (leaves only)

Preheat the oven to 200°F (95°C).

HERE'S WHAT YOU DO

1 Line a baking sheet with parchment paper. Beat the egg whites with an electric mixer until soft peaks start to form (they should partially stand up but still droop over at the top).

2 Turn off the mixer and add the cream of tartar, vanilla, and half of the sugar. Mix until combined, then add the remaining sugar.

3 Keep beating the mixture until the peaks stiffen and stand up straight when you pull the beaters out.

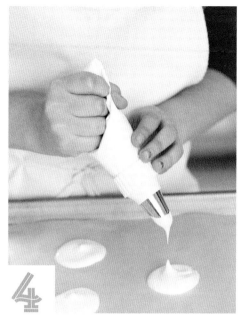

4 Spoon the meringue into a pastry bag fitted with a large tip. Or fill a quart-size ziplock plastic bag and snip off a corner. Pipe silver dollar–size rounds onto the parchment.

5 Make an indent in the center of each meringue with a spoon handle. Bake the meringues for about 1 hour 20 minutes. They should be crisp but not brown.

6 Remove the baking sheet from the oven and slide the meringues off the parchment paper onto a rack. Once they have cooled completely, fill the nests with whipped cream, berries, and mint leaves.

7 Serve immediately. You can store unfilled meringues in an airtight container at room temperature for 5 days.

CREATIVE COOKS!

MERINGUE LOLLIPOPS

Food on a stick is always fun. Why not bake meringue lollipops? Set ice-pop or lollipop sticks on a parchment paper–lined baking sheet about 2 inches apart.

Pipe the meringue mixture in a swirling pattern on one end of each stick. Add rainbow sprinkles. Bake the meringues following the directions in step 5.

MAISIE'S CARROT CUPCAKES

Makes 24 cupcakes

You may think that carrots are just for snacks and salads. Think again! Carrots taste terrific in desserts, too. What better way to eat your veggies than in a cupcake?

Here's What You Need

- 2 cups flour
- 1 tablespoon cinnamon
- 2 teaspoons baking powder
- 1 teaspoon baking soda
- ¾ teaspoon salt
- 1¾ cups sugar
- 1½ cups vegetable oil
- 4 eggs
- 3 cups grated carrots (about 9 carrots)

Preheat the oven to 350°F (180°C).

HERE'S WHAT YOU DO

1 Line two 12-cup muffin pans with paper liners. Sift the flour, cinnamon, baking powder, baking soda, and salt into a large bowl. Set aside.

2 Blend the sugar, oil, and eggs in a bowl with an electric mixer until fluffy.

3 Mix in the grated carrots until combined.

4 Add the dry ingredients to the wet ingredients and mix thoroughly.

5 Use an ice cream scoop to fill each muffin cup about halfway.

6 Bake the cupcakes for 25 minutes, until light brown on top. Remove them from the oven and cool completely on a rack before frosting. (See frosting recipe on page 172.)

FRESH from the oven!

BAKER'S SECRETS FLOUR Sugar

If you want to learn how to bake like the pros, try these tips!

* Sift your flour, baking powder, and other dry ingredients together.

* Line your baking sheets and cake pans with parchment paper.

* Use an ice cream scoop to fill cupcake pans.

* Buy a cake decorating kit with disposable pastry bags and basic icing tips.

* Make your baked goods from scratch instead of using mixes.

* Check for doneness: If a toothpick comes out clean, your cake is done!

* Freeze or refrigerate your cakes before you frost them (it's easier and you avoid getting crumbs in your frosting).

* To prevent flour from flying around your kitchen while you use a stand mixer, carefully wrap a dish towel around the bowl and hold it in the back, keeping fingers out of the way.

CREAM CHEESE FROSTING

DELISH

Makes 2 cups

It's fun to color some of this frosting orange and green with food coloring to make decorative carrots on top of each cupcake.

Here's What You Need

8 ounces cream cheese, softened
4 tablespoons butter, softened
3½ cups confectioners' sugar
1 teaspoon vanilla extract
Food coloring (orange and green)

SPECIAL EQUIPMENT
Pastry bags with icing tips

HERE'S WHAT YOU DO

1 Beat the cream cheese and butter together in a bowl with an electric mixer.

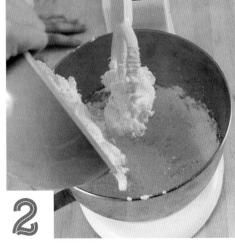

2 Slowly add the confectioners' sugar and vanilla. Beat until the frosting is smooth and creamy.

TIP: If the spreader becomes too gooey, dip it in a glass of warm water every once in a while to make it easier to spread the frosting.

3 Frost the cooled cupcakes with a butter knife.

4 Divide the remaining frosting into two bowls. Add orange food coloring to one bowl and green food coloring to the other. Mix well. Transfer the frosting to pastry bags.

5 Use the writing tips—a slightly larger one for the carrots and a smaller one for the leaves.

6 Practice a few carrots on a piece of waxed paper, then make one on each cupcake.

7 Start with a big squish of orange frosting, then draw the tip of the bag toward you, letting up on the pressure so the carrot comes to a point.

8 Add three green leaves and your carrot patch is all set!

INDEX

BONUS PULL-OUT FEATURES!

PLACE CARDS

Fold them along the center line and the decoration will pop up. Fold them the other way to reuse.

STICKERS & LABELS

Some are meant to be folded onto a long toothpick and used to decorate sliders, sandwiches, cupcakes, or anything you can think of!

GAME CARDS

What's a good meal without good conversation around the table? Tear out the cards and shuffle them into a bowl or jar. Have everyone pick a card and see where it leads you.

IF YOU WERE A FOOD, what would you be?

Which flavor do you like better, **CHOCOLATE** or **VANILLA**

Are you a **LEFTY** or a **RIGHTY**? Try eating your dinner with your fork or spoon in the other hand!

RECIPE CARDS

When you run out of these, you can use index cards decorated with stickers.

THIS COOKING KIT belongs to:

_____'S COOKING KIT

MADE FROM SCRATCH

SPREAD the LOVE

This LUNCH BELONGS TO:

This LUNCH belongs to:

MORE PLEASE!

FRESH

Made with my VERY OWN hands

JUST Roll with it.

to: made for you with from

a TREAT for you!

From:

To:

FRESH from the oven!

HOT OFF THE GRILL

LET'S GET COOKIN'

SEASONED with LOVE

'S

CINNAMON
SUGAR

'S
HOMEMADE
PEANUT
BUTTER

'S
EASY-PEASY
APPLE
SAUCE

'S
GARDEN
SALSA

'S
MEAN
GREEN
GUACAMOLE

'S
Perfect
PESTO

'S
MICROWAVE
POPCORN

'S
BALL of
YUM!

'S
HOT
COGOA
MIX

Balsamic Vinaigrette

GRAB-and-GO GRANOLA BAR

GRAB-and-GO GRANOLA BAR

GRAB-and-GO GRANOLA BAR

GRAB-and-GO GRANOLA BAR

Maple Mustard Dressing

SUGAR and SPICE

SMART COOKIE

I LOVE Chocolate ♥♥♥

Creamy Gorgonzola Dressing

SWEET!
sweet!

WWW!
Mmm!

Scones

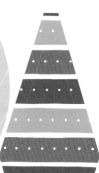

Lemon · Parmesan Dressing

Home on the RANCH ~Dressing~

Enjoy
Enjoy

DELISH
DELISH

LET'S EAT!
LET'S EAT!

YUM
YUM

Name a **YELLOW** food you ate this week.

Which flavor do you like better, **CHOCOLATE** or **VANILLA**?

What's the **BEST MEAL** you've ever eaten?

Are you a **LEFTY** or a **RIGHTY**? Try eating your dinner with your fork or spoon in the other hand!

What's the **WEIRDEST** thing you've ever eaten?

How many ingredients went into your dinner?

Name a food that starts with the **LETTER A**! Now try B, C, D, and all the way to Z!

What recipe can you make on your own? What recipe do you feel most proud of?

Name 6 different **FRUITS** (or **NUTS** or **VEGGIES** or **DESSERTS**)!

IF YOU WERE A FOOD, what would you be?

What food did you dislike at first, but now you like?

Name a **RED** food you ate this week.

Name a **GREEN** food you ate this week.

Are you a vegetarian?

Do you know anyone who is?

If you could invite **ANYONE IN THE WORLD** to dinner, who would it be? Why?

If you opened a restaurant, what would you call it?

What would you serve?

If you had a **KITCHEN SUPER-POWER**, what would it be?

What is your earliest **FOOD MEMORY**?

What food are you **AFRAID TO TRY**? Why?

What are your **favorite** and **least** favorite **KITCHEN CHORES**?

Name an **ORANGE** food you ate this week.

I am **CRAVING** ——— **RIGHT NOW!**

Have you ever planted a garden?

What veggies did you grow?

NAME 4 FOODS that are in your fridge right now. **NO PEEKING!**

RECIPE FOR: _____

WHAT YOU DO:

WHAT YOU NEED:

YIELD: _____

RECIPE FOR: _____

WHAT YOU DO:

WHAT YOU NEED:

YIELD: _____

RECIPE FOR: _____

WHAT YOU DO:

WHAT YOU NEED:

YIELD: _____

RECIPE FOR: _____

WHAT YOU DO:

WHAT YOU NEED:

YIELD: _____

RECIPE FOR: _____

WHAT YOU DO:

WHAT YOU NEED:

YIELD: _____

RECIPE FOR: _____

WHAT YOU DO:

WHAT YOU NEED:

YIELD: _____

WHY THIS RECIPE ROCKS!

I GOT THIS RECIPE FROM:

NOTES:

WHY THIS RECIPE ROCKS!

I GOT THIS RECIPE FROM:

NOTES:

WHY THIS RECIPE ROCKS!

I GOT THIS RECIPE FROM:

NOTES:

WHY THIS RECIPE ROCKS!

I GOT THIS RECIPE FROM:

NOTES:

WHY THIS RECIPE ROCKS!

I GOT THIS RECIPE FROM:

NOTES:

WHY THIS RECIPE ROCKS!

I GOT THIS RECIPE FROM:

NOTES: